Recovery from Addictions and Compulsive Behavior

A Journaling-Based Guide to Becoming Your Best Self and Having a Life Worth Living

Andy Matzner, lcsw

Disclaimer

This book is made available with the understanding that the author is not engaged in offering specific medical, psychological, or emotional advice. Nor is anything in this book designed to be a diagnosis, prescription or cure for any kind of specific medical, psychological or emotional problem. The information, ideas and suggestions in this book are not intended to be a substitute for professional advice.

Each person is unique and this book cannot take those individual differences into account. Any person suffering from a serious mental illness should consult with a doctor or licensed psychotherapist before practicing the exercises in this book. In addition, before you make any drastic changes in your diet, please consult with your healthcare provider. The author therefore accepts no liability or responsibility for any results, outcomes or consequences of the use of content, ideas or concepts expressed or provided in this book.

Enlightenment is: Eat when you are hungry, sleep when you are tired.

Zen saying

There are only two mistakes a person can make along the road to truth: Not going all the way, and not starting.

the Buddha

The purpose of life is not to be happy – but to matter, to be productive, to be useful, to have it make some difference that you have lived at all.

Leo Rosten

The first rule of holes: When you are in one, stop digging.

Molly Ivins

In order to be empowered to change anything, we must be clear about what we gain from staying stuck. In therapy, this gain is referred to as secondary gain. *Secondary gains are the benefits people get from NOT overcoming a problem.*

Terri Cole

Pain brought me to mindfulness, not any desire to reach nirvana or pop out of any chrysalis. It was "unlearning" certain habits and thought patterns hard-wired in my brain and walking through my pain, rather than avoiding it, that ultimately put me on a joyful journey of self-discovery.

George Mumford

What stories did we acquire as children, what marching orders did we receive to serve in the remaining chapters of our history? Were we to be the unseen child, the fixer, the scapegoat, the marginalized? How do those stories persist in the present?

James Hollis

Our experience quite literally is defined by our assumptions about life...We make stories about the world and to a large degree live out their plots. What our lives are like depends to a great extent on the script we consciously, or more likely, unconsciously, have adopted.

Carol Pearson

How do we accept...that we are not our history but our unfolding journey?

James Hollis

Note on terminology

Compulsion: An irresistible impulse to engage in a behavior. Compulsions often have a ritualistic aspect and typically serve to reduce anxiety. A characteristic of compulsions is that people usually do not derive pleasure in acting them out.

Addiction: The compulsive need to use a substance (such as alcohol or coffee) or engage in a behavior (such as running or gambling) in order to create a change in one's state of consciousness. With an addiction, it becomes more difficult as time passes to achieve that initial change in state. This tolerance is known as *dependence* and leads a person to use more of a substance or engage in more of a behavior in order to achieve the same effects as before. As an addiction progresses, one of its hallmarks is that the person knows it is harmful but becomes unable or unwilling to stop.

Although some people argue that addictions and compulsions are two very different things, for the purpose of this book I use both terms interchangeably and alongside one another. This is because what both have in common is that they are behaviors that originally served a positive purpose (and may continue to do so). However, what makes something "addictive" or "compulsive" is that it is interfering with a person's ability to function and is negatively impacting the quality of their life.

Most importantly, a person with a compulsion or addiction feels that they do not have any control over their decision-making process and behavior when it comes to a particular substance or activity. That is, it has become difficult – if not apparently impossible – to change and break free. The price of doing so is such a negative one (in terms of experiencing pain, anxiety, fear, physical withdrawal, boredom, stress, sadness, existential emptiness) that the addictive or compulsive behavior seems like the only alternative that makes sense. I wrote this book to help you overcome that challenge by offering you the skills, strategies and information that will make it easier for your to leave your addictions and compulsions behind.

I offer you a path out.

This book is dedicated to everyone I met while
working at the Virginia Alcohol Safety Action Program.
You showed me the way.

Please Read!

This book is journal-based and as such is full of questions and writing prompts for you to reflect on and answer. This is because in order to truly become the best version of yourself, you will first have to become an expert on yourself: Who are you? Where do you come from? How has your past influenced your present? Where do you truly need to go from here?

Therefore your progress along the route to recovery is directly based on your doing the work. Really doing the work. No excuses. Which means not just reading through this book, but actually carving out the time to sit down and write. It doesn't matter how much. Just that you write *something*.

This is an opportunity for you to to be honest with yourself, develop important insights, and chart a course for the future that is free of the emotional, mental, physical and spiritual anguish you have been so used to. A future that will allow you to fulfill your potential and have a life worth living.

So please buy a notebook or journal to accompany you on this journey.

It will be one of the best investments you've ever made.

You're worth it.

P.S. Take your time. After all, Rome wasn't built in a day. And be sure that you have emotional support as you go through this book – you'll be digging pretty deep.

CONTENTS

Introduction

Drug or alcohol dependence. Eating disorders, including anorexia, bulimia and emotional eating. Compulsive gambling. Self-injury. Pornography. Co-dependent relationships. The inability to tear oneself away from the television set or the computer or video games...

The details don't matter. The common thread is that we become obsessed with something – a substance, a behavior – which in turn negatively impacts the quality of our lives (whether we're aware of it or not). We lose control.

It used to be that addictions were considered a moral failing, a weakness of spirit. And so willpower was the key to recovery. In more recent times, addictive behavior has become thought of as a disease, based on genetics. One we're born with and die with, no matter how many years sober. Abstinence is key, as a single drink can push a person with 30 years recovery instantly back into their addiction.

Yet even more recently some researchers have questioned the "disease model" of addictive and compulsive behaviors by asking: Is it true that people are simply fated to become addicts due to their faulty biology? Could there be other causes that lead someone to use?

The answer to that question forms the basis of this book. It has been my experience that the roots of many people's addictive or compulsive behavior lie in a desire to obtain some sort of *relief*. The form of this self-medication will be different for each of us because we are all unique beings, with different psychological, cultural, familial, and physiological backgrounds and sets of experiences.

So whether it's alcohol, gambling or emotional eating, by examining our lives – especially our childhood – it becomes possible to discover the healing role the substance or behavior originally played. What ended up becoming an addiction or compulsive behavior originally started out as:

- a way to respond to trauma or loss.

- a distraction.

- a form of self-punishment to alleviate guilt.

- a way to feel more relaxed or comfortable in social situations.

- a strategy to alleviate the symptoms of depression, anxiety, or posttraumatic stress disorder.

- a quick fix to calm overwhelming emotions (whether positive or negative), such as fear, anger, or excitement.

- a tool to regulate an unbalanced biological system.

- a way to receive caregiving responses from others.

- a strategy to keep people at a distance.

- a way to create the illusion of being in control.

- a solution to alleviate physical pain.

- a remedy to address an overwhelming feeling of emptiness.

Sometimes addictions and compulsions continue to provide the relief for which they were originally intended. But more often they just end up becoming problems unto themselves. They now hold us back from our potential, from the life we deserve to have. In our hearts, we know that our addiction doesn't serve us. That our compulsive behavior is only a temporary fix. This is a road we've walked down countless times, knowing exactly to where it leads: Nowhere. Yet we continue, time after time. And we won't stop until we discover, for ourselves, a more compelling alternative.

So it's important to emphasize the following: Even if we treat our addiction or compulsion by going to AA or NA or psychotherapy or a sober living house, none of that will matter if we ignore the original reason for developing the addiction. As long as the necessary deep healing doesn't occur, as long as the original wound continues to bleed, a person will always be in seach of relief.

Therefore, we might want to ask ourselves how the compulsive behavior originally provided that relief – and acknowledge that it typically still does so, no matter how temporary it might be. So the goal is not to simply swap one compulsion for another; quitting drinking only to get obsessive about working out doesn't solve the problem. No, the goal is to fully recover from addictive behavior – for good.

And that is why I have written this book. To give you the chance to explore the roots of what is driving your addiction or compulsion in order that you may heal once and for all. My desire is that you become able to change your relationship with your addictive behavior. The bottle of beer, the box of cookies, the razor blade, the computer, the casino….these will no longer represent salvation. Rather, you will see them for what they simply are – no more and no less. It won't make sense to use them for relief because of the healing work you've already done. It won't make sense to treat yourself poorly. It won't make sense to use something external in order to give yourself what you already have as your birthright.

THE PATH TO RECOVERY

What does it mean to "recover" from an addiction or compulsion?

For me, recovery is reflected in a life that is well-lived. One that is worthwhile, meaningful, full of purpose. It's a journey that certainly never ends, but it's one in which we are in control, acting in a conscious and deliberate manner, instead of being at the beck and call of an addiction or compulsion.

On this journey to recovery, we develop insight about our past by exploring important questions:

Who am I? Why am I the way we am? Why do I act and *react* the way I do? And most importanly, What am I capable of? How might I best fulfill my potential?

As you make your way through this book you will have the opportunity to rediscover yourself. Who you were before the trauma. Before the addiction. Before you lost touch with what really mattered to you...

You will learn how to accept yourself for who you are as you rebuild your identity, letting go of shame and self-judgment. You'll realize that you can be vulnerable. That you can be hopeful about your future. That you have both the duty and ability to be responsible for your own life. *That* is recovery.

You will discover those things that you were never taught growing up: How to manage your emotions. How to experience the love and support of other people. How to love yourself. How to find and nurture those people, places, things and activities that truly speak to your soul.

You will have the opportunity to redefine your sense of self. You've learned a great deal traveling your path. It's hard-earned wisdom. And now you get to use it as your guide.

The payoff is getting off the hamster wheel that you know too well. It's being able to live in a deliberate manner, being guided by your core values and beliefs. *Responding* instead of *reacting*. On your deathbed you'll be able to look back and truly believe that it mattered you were here.

The positive changes you'll be experiencing as you go through this program will change your life forever – if you give yourself permission to do what's involved. I think you'll be very proud of what you have accomplished once you've worked your way through this book. Certainly, like anything else worthwhile, it will take commitment, persistence, and patience. Plus the faith that you're doing the right thing for yourself. But just the fact that you're reading these words indicates to me that you're ready to get started.

In order to recover from your addiction or compulsion and start the next chapter of your life, two things are necessary. First, the opportunity to explore your past so that you can come to understand who you really are and why you've made the decisions you have. That's why there are so many journaling questions in this book. Second, practical strategies that will help you become healthy: physically, mentally, emotionally and spiritually. And when I use the word "healthy," I'm referring to its original sense, of being "whole."

My aim with each chapter in this book is to give you the information and the skills to become the best possible version of yourself. So think of this as a guide, like a textbook for the school of life. It's what we should have learned in high school.

Luckily it's not too late.

***

Now it is time to truly begin! We will start with some journaling. Please find a safe, comfortable space and make sure that you won't be disturbed, as you'll need to give yourself enough time to answer the questions I have for you.

Don't over-think things; just follow your intuition and allow yourself to notice and then express what emerges into your consciousness.

As you think about starting this journey and what it might mean for you...

What excites you about what lays ahead?

What concerns do you have?

How will your daily schedule reflect your commitment to this book?

What will you have to stop doing in order to have the energy to engage in this program?

What are the implications for you if you decide to put this off?

How does it feel to be in uncharted territory?

When presented with something new, do you find yourself being open or skeptical?

How do you feel about taking risks in general?

How does it actually feel to take a risk?

What message can you tell yourself that will allow you to "feel the fear and do it anyway"?

What kind of emotional support system can you set up for yourself as you do this work?

Inventory #1

Let's start by taking a detailed inventory of your life. How are things going? Please assign a number to each of the scales below, with 1 representing the pretty awful side of things and 10 being your ideal. If a an area doesn't apply to you (for example, school), then just leave it blank.

Sleep

1--|------------------10

Family Relationships

1-----|--10

Intimate Relationship(s)

1--------------------|--10

Relationship with Children

1--10

Physical Health

1-|---10

Mental Health

1-|---10

Relationship with God / Higher Power

1-|---10

Spirituality / Religion

1--|---10

Work/Career

1---|----------10

Finances

1--|------------------------10

Leisure Time / Relaxation

1--|10

Hobbies / Things you do for fun

1--10

Relationship with Food

1--10

Education / School

1--10

Relationships with Friends

1--10

Legal Issues

1--10

Energy Level

1--10

Optimism about the Future

1--10

Don't be discouraged if you're not where you'd like to be with your life. What's important is to begin with a base-line idea of where you're currently at. As you work your way through this book your numbers will certainly begin to improve.

Please answer the following questions in your journal:

It seems like I often end up...

I'm always...

I never...

I often notice that...

When I think about how my relationships are with other people, it always seems like...

Even though I often try ---, it usually seems that --- happens instead.

Looking back on my life, some of my most painful memories were when:

Looking back on my life, some of my happiest memories were when:

If I'm honest with myself, what is something I have been avoiding that I need to do as soon as possible?

It's hard for me to....

It's easy for me to...

***

Thinking about the journey you have taken to get to this point in your life, how would you fill in the following?

This is a story of a --- who ---

Looking back on my life, I now understand ----

I will never understand ---

I have made peace with the fact that ---

In the future, I would like to be living a life in which I am ---

As you think about your future:

What does "recovery" look like for you? How would you define that term?

How would you like the roles that you currently play in your life to change?

How would you like your relationship with fear to change?

How would you like to change the relationship you have with the expectations of others?

How will your past story influence your new story?

What will you be doing to empower yourself?

What will your relationship be with spirituality? How will you be connecting with a Higher Power (however you might define that)?

What will you be doing to create happiness / peace / fulfillment?

What will be making your life meaningful?

What patterns would you like to see happening in your new story?

What adjectives described your life when you were tied to your addiction or compulsive behavior?

What adjectives would you like to use to to describe yourself/your life in your new story?

What will be working well for you in your new life? What will you be doing so that those things are working well?

What has worked well for you in the past? How will you continue to incorporate it into your new life?

What hasn't worked well for you in the past? How will you avoid repeating those patterns?

In order to create a new life that is empowering for you:

What obstacles will you face? How will you successfully overcome them?

What must you release?

What must you learn?

What skills must you develop?

What will you do to get through difficult times?

Whom must you forgive? What is the benefit of doing so?

What compromises will you be willing to make?

What commitments will you need to make? With whom? Why will those commitments be important?

***

What disappointments or hurts from the past do you still have strong feelings about?

What is the advantage to holding on to resentment, anger, disappointment and/or regret? What is the disadvantage?

***

Do you have clarity about your dreams and goals? Your heart's desire? If not, what will allow you to gain that clarity? What do you need to do?

CHAPTER 1

How to Change (Or Not)

We cannot solve our problems with the same thinking we used when we created them.

Albert Einstein

To heal a suffering one must experience it to the full.

Marcel Proust

We cannot change anything until we accept it. Condemnation does not liberate, it oppresses.

Carl Jung

True mastery can be gained by letting things go their own way. It can't be gained by interfering.

Lao Tzu

Whether it is a New Year's resolution or the latest diet, forcing ourselves to change because we "should" typically proves frustrating and disappointing. Changing because you *have to* rarely works long-term because this type of change is dependent on **willpower**. In effect, you are at war with yourself. There is a part of you who wants to change, while at the same time there is another part of you that wants to stay the same. This forces a person to expend a great deal of effort in creating and maintaining change. Because that tension is always present, true change is impossible.

So here is something to consider: What if instead of trying to force yourself to make a change, you first took some time to settle into your current self? That is, what if you stopped trying to be something you are not, and made a decision to simply accept yourself as you are, today? By doing so, the energy that you've been expending in the battle between trying to change and resisting change suddenly becomes available for other, more productive, uses.

Of course you might naturally ask, How does "giving up and settling in" actually create change? Well, I have found that **when the time is ripe**, change will happen **naturally** – without being forced. The essential ingredient is your intention. Your intention to be open. Your intention to follow your intuition. Your intention to let this process unfold in its own time, without pushing it.

My belief is that a heightened awareness of our current state is what actually allows change to occur. That is, in order to step into our future, we must **first** be fully engaged in the reality of our present life. This means that change must begin from our life as it is, not from how we would like it to be.

Therefore, your first task, when it comes to change, is to consider and then accept the reality of your life, both past and present. It is important to make peace with and take responsibility for your past and present choices. In doing so, you can then be fully aware of your current position in life.

Arnold Beisser writes:

> *Change can occur when [a person] abandons, at least for the moment, what he would like to become and attempts to be what he is. The premise is that one must stand in one place in order to have firm footing to move and that it is difficult or impossible to move without that footing.*

As you explore who you *think* we are, and then discover who you *really* are, you'll soon reach the deepest core of your being. This is why I have filled this book with introspective journaling exercises. You will encounter questions that will make you think deeply and honestly about your life, questions that will compel you to take inventory. I want to challenge the values and assumptions that have guided you up to this point; the ones that have influenced the relationship you currently have with your addiction/compulsion – a partnership I assume you would like to change.

The journaling work you do during this program will allow you to discover – and discard – those parts of yourself (ideas, beliefs, personas) that no longer serve your best interests. As you consider your life, you will understand that you have unlived potential just waiting to be realized. Think of the resulting emptiness as fertile soil, in which space has been created for your true self to emerge and grow.

But facing our reality is typically not easy. Because the process makes us feel vulnerable, we generally avoid it. However, the process of going back so that we can go forward, while painful, is essential to our lives if we truly desire peace.

So this is the paradox of change. First, we must release our conscious desire to change. Next, we must fully embrace our present selves – who and where we are now. With that awareness, we can face our wounds and fears. We can dissolve what is blocking us and learn to live in the here and now. Then – and only then – by recognizing and dealing with unfinished business from the past and in the present, can we begin to consider, and perhaps even follow, other potential paths that resonate more deeply within us.

It is only when our delusions have been stripped away and we have our feet firmly planted in the reality of our lives, that we can gradually begin to move forward again, embracing our possibilities and our futures because we are no longer encumbered by the baggage of our past. With the resulting awareness and insight, the change that had been impossible for us will emerge spontaneously and authentically.

That is, we will **intuitively** make the decisions that are right for us. No effort or force required!

The most important thing to remember is that when you are ready to change, you will. Not sooner and not later. So it is fine if you don't yet feel compelled to make changes in your life. Don't force yourself to be somewhere that you don't *yet* belong. After all, change can be scary because it is unpredictable. And if the perceived pain of change outweighs the pain of staying the same, you might spend a long time simply thinking about changing without taking any concrete action. Which is OK, if that is where you are.

A way to make sense of this is to consider your location on the **Stages of Change** model (developed by psychologist James Prochaska). These five stages describe the process a person passes through on their way to creating and maintaining change. People move from stage to stage organically, in their own time, when they are ready. A person can't be forced to move from one stage to another, either by guilt or by other people. The most important thing is to accept our current stage, and recognize that we will move to the next stage when the time is right.

- The **precontemplation** stage is when you are unaware there is a problem, and therefore you have no desire to change.

- You move into the **contemplation** stage when you begin to think that there *might* be a something in your life that needs to change. During this time, you'll be on the fence about whether or not to commit to changing.

- In the **preparation** stage you've made up your mind to take action. You begin to take concrete steps to prepare to make a change, gearing up for doing the actual work necessary to accomplish your goal.

- During the **Action** Stage you are actively engaged in new behaviors related to achieving your goal. You are consciously creating concrete changes in your life and are fully committed to changing.

- In the **maintenance** stage, you have accomplished your goal and have been living a lifestyle that is congruent with your values for an extended amount of time.

- **Relapse** refers to occasions when you slip back into old, unhealthy habits. When this occurs, it is time to revisit your core values and learn from the experience of relapsing so that it doesn't happen again. (for me, relapse is a judgment-free zone and nothing to be ashamed about)

The journaling exercises in this book are vital because they are designed to create the opportunity for cultivating self-knowledge. Through introspection and self-inquiry, you can begin to create the conditions for change to occur naturally. This is because *the right questions* are the most effective tools for moving a person from the **precontemplation** stage to the **action** stage. Fran Peavey writes:

> *Questioning is a basic tool for rebellion. It breaks open the stagnant hardened shells of the present, revealing ambiguity and opening up fresh options to be explored...Questioning can change your entire life. It can uncover hidden power and stifled dreams inside of you...things you may have denied for many years.*

When you learn about yourself, become comfortable with who you are, and unconditionally accept yourself (for better or worse), then – paradoxically – you will begin to move in a direction that is right for you.

So before you focus on making concrete changes in your life I would like you to simply spend some time thinking about yourself and your life (past and present). There will also be times when I will also ask you to use your imagination to think about the future. I believe that doing all of this will lead you to exactly where you need to go. In fact, that is one of the main ideas of this book – that introspection leads to self-acceptance than then leads to a whole-hearted desire to change. The effort you spend now learning more about yourself will dramatically change the relationship you currently have with yourself and your ability to move forward in your recovery.

***

Now I'd like you to find a safe, comfortable space where you can be alone and undisturbed as you write in your journal. Take some deep breaths so you can clear your mind. Your goal is to access your intuitive voice. This is the part of you that resides deep in your soul and is just waiting to express itself to you. It is you being honest with yourself, simply because it is the right time.

Do you remember the first time you used a substance that later you'd become addcited to or engaged in what would become a compulsive behavior? What happened? How did it make you feel?

What have been some things people have told you about your compulsive behavior or substance use?

Please make a list of events that stick in your memory that are related to your substance usage or compulsions.

Now let's shift to the first person; please fill in the following in your journal:

- o   What my addiction / compulsive behavior says about me:

- o   How it makes me feel:

- o   What I believe about it:

- o   What I have learned from it:

- o   What I could still learn from it:

- o   What or whom have I lost in my life, due to my substance abuse / compulsive behavior?

- o   How might I grieve and/or honor each of those losses?

- o   What or who in my life has become more important as a result of my substance abuse / compulsive behavior?

- o   Is there another way to view my addiction / compulsion? Could it mean something other than what I currently think it means?

- o   If my addiction / compulsion could speak, what message would it give me?

Next, I'd like you to conduct a cost/benefit analysis of staying the same in your life versus making some changes. To begin, divide up a piece of paper in your journal into four quarters.

In the first, please write: **Advantages of staying the same**

In the second: **Disadvantages staying the same**

In the third: **Advantages of creating changes in my life that will support my recovery**

In the fourth: **Disadvantages of creating changes in my life that will support my recovery**

Once you have filled in each of the four quadrants, take some time to study what you have written. What are your lists telling you? Do they give you a new perspective about the current quality of your life? The potential future quality of your life? Does what you have written affect your commitment to begin living your life differently? If so, how?

What do you think it might cost you in the future if you do not make a change in your daily habits?

What costs have you already experienced in the past due to your addiction / compulsion?

If you were to make a change, what positive things do you think might occur in the future?

If you were to make a change, what negative things might occur?

How would your changes positively affect the people around you?

How might your changes negatively affect people in your life?

Imagine that it is many years from now and you are nearing the end of your life. Use your imagination and pretend that you had decided NOT to make any changes in your life.

1. What were the consequences of your decision on your health?

2. On your relationships?

3. On your sense of well-being?

4. On your body?

5. On your dreams?

It is five years from now, having made the decision to deal with your substance use / compulsive behavior. And you've been successful. Close your eyes and use your imagination...How does that future feel and look to you? What do you notice? What's going on around you? Are you glad you made the decisions you did? Are you satisfied with the changes that have occurred in your life? Why?

CHAPTER 2

Mindfulness

Question: *What one word should I carry with me for the rest of my life?*
Peter Bloom

Answer: *Observation!*
Milton Erickson

The moment one gives close attention to anything, even a blade of grass, it becomes a mysterious, awesome, indescribably magnificent world in itself.

Henry Miller

Facing the bluntness of reality is the highest form of sanity and enlightened vision….Devotion proceeds through various stages of unmasking until we reach the point of seeing the world directly and simply without imposing our fabrications…

Chogyam Trungpa Rinpoche

Mindfulness isn't difficult, we just need to remember to do it.

Sharon Salzberg

Mindfulness will be a cornerstone of your recovery because it influences every aspect of your life. This skill comes first because everything that follows depends on it. But what exactly does "mindfulness" entail?

The concept of mindfulness includes the ideas of:

- Awareness of the present moment
- Focused attention
- Acceptance

Working with mindfulness, you will begin to pay attention deliberately in order to consider *where* you place your attention, and *how* you go about doing things. You'll also learn to check in with yourself in order to discover your motivations for action. "I'm craving a drink. Hmmm….let me take a moment and pay attention to what I'm actually thinking and feeling instead of rushing to distract myself."

As you practice this skill, you will learn that instead of being trapped in the past or future, you can access a sense of freedom that can only be experienced by living in the present. This is because when it comes to reality, the present moment is where health and healing are to be found. The "**now**" is where spontaneity, acceptance, and compassion live. It is the space in which you are able to take deliberate action for your own benefit.

We have little control over the past or the future. However, we often base our decision-making on prior experiences or expectations about the future. Indeed, things that happened to us in the past generally influence how we experience the present (and think about the future). Our beliefs, ideals, self-images, memories, desires, hopes, prejudices, attitudes, assumptions, and accumulated knowledge all combine to create the lens through which we see – and interact with – ourselves and the world around us. And that lens colors our response to everything that we experience. The result is that we lose the ability to respond appropriately to situations as they arise. Instead of being able to act spontaneously, our past conditioning greatly limits our choices in the present.

We can break these chains to the past, however, when we become aware of our current thoughts, feelings, and body sensations.

Through mindfulness we gain freedom as we realize a type of clarity that allows us to see things as they are, not as we fear or hope they are. From this we then can create authentic and meaningful connections with what is happening around us. And that is vital, because we can create change *only* in the present moment.

So a major goal of mindfulness training is to develop the ability to see things as they really are, uninfluenced by our past conditioning. By acting deliberately instead of reactively, we can experience ourselves spontaneously in the moment, as we get in touch with our true, essential nature. But in order to do that, we must first become conscious of how we avoid being present in our daily life. This means gaining an understanding of how our past conditioning influences (and limits) our choices in the present. As we become students of our own minds, we can use the knowledge we gain to escape our habitual reactions, thereby freeing ourselves to make more appropriate responses in life.

At the same time, we can use our mindfulness skills to notice how often we become disengaged from what is going on around us. It is easy to be distracted. Our pace of life usually is fast and we are often forced to multitask. Instead of fully being in the present moment, we are in multiple places at once. By checking in with ourselves and noticing that we are not present, we can recognize what is happening. That knowledge then allows us shift our attention back to what is going on right in front of us.

For example, consider food and eating. Think about how often you actually pay close attention to the process of choosing, preparing and eating food. It is easy to eat an entire meal and not really taste even a single bite! It is also easy to prepare and eat an entire meal based on habit rather than true feelings of hunger.

But when you begin to pay close attention to what you are putting on your plate and into your mouth, you will experience a connection with food and eating that will be both empowering and satisfying. Instead of being an unconscious process, it will become meaningful. And when you notice how your body feels after a meal, you will gain important information about how food truly affects you.

I have divided the concept of mindfulness into six main components in order to simplify it. Remember, your commitment to learning this skill is an investment in the quality of the rest of your life!

PAYING ATTENTION

This is a core aspect of mindfulness. To pay attention means *slowing down* enough so that you are able to notice what is going on around you. It means committing to a pace that is the opposite of *rushing*. And as you slow yourself down and move deliberately through your life, all you need to do is observe your surroundings. Sounds simple, doesn't it? But this is a way of living that many of us are divorced from, because our minds usually are "somewhere else."

The easiest way to tap into this aspect of mindfulness is to pay attention to each of your senses. Shift your focus to what you **see** around you. What you **hear**. How things **feel** to your body. When you are eating, notice the texture of your food, both in your hands and in your mouth. Be attentive to what you **taste** and how it **smells**. And then focus on how your body feels after your meal.

Paying attention also means focusing on what is going on inside of you throughout the day. Notice how you are breathing. Where in your chest is your breath? Is it deep or shallow? Observe your mood and any emotions you might be experiencing. What are you feeling? If you notice that you are not in the present moment, then where are you? Thinking about the past? Imagining the future? Are you distracted? How so? Why?

The most important thing you can do with this skill is to notice – and be curious about – where your attention goes. Curiosity is a wonderful characteristic to have. Just pretend you are a stranger observing yourself, one who is interested in why you are doing what you are doing. This will give you all the information you need about your current state of being. And once you begin to recognize unhelpful patterns, then you can begin to change.

TIP: If you find that you are distracted and are having a difficult time focusing attention on yourself or your surroundings, try one of the following ideas to help re-orient yourself:

- o Notice what is directly in front of you and pay attention to it.

- o Imagine it's the *first time* you are looking at or experiencing something. Really be curious!

- o Pick one of your five senses and focus especially on it.

- o Notice your breath and follow it as you inhale and exhale.

- o Pick a part of your body and pay attention to it. For example, notice your hand, your fingers, your fingertips, your nails...

- o Tell yourself, either out-loud or silently, "Focus!" or "Slow down!"

CONCENTRATION

This form of mindfulness refers to committing one's attention directly to whatever task is at hand. Connected to the skill of paying attention, this refers to the ability to filter out distractions, and be completely present while engaged in doing something. The idea of focusing on one thing at a time may sound easy, but as I mentioned above, our pace of life often makes this difficult to put into practice.

When you develop the skill of concentration, you will find that you will be able to truly inhabit the present moment. Some people refer to this as being in the "zone," where time actually stands still. For example, when we eat, it is very easy to be distracted. If we are eating and reading, watching TV, or thinking about other things, we often become disconnected from what we are putting into our bodies. This lack of connection means we are unaware of exactly what we are eating and how much we are consuming. Paying attention to that process and concentrating fully on each bite of food will give you control over this important part of your life.

TIP: The best way to develop your capacity for paying attention and concentration is through **meditation**. There are several ways to meditate. In one kind of meditation practice, the goal is to focus on a single thing while sitting comfortably in a place where you won't be disturbed. For example, you can simply follow your breath in and out. Or you can choose a word like "love" or "peace" and silently repeat it over and over in your mind or out loud. You could also use any stationary object (like a flower, a bowl, a burning candle or even a spot on the wall) as your focal point.

My recommendation is to use a digital timer on your phone (with a pleasant-sounding alarm) so you don't have to worry about keeping track of time while you meditate. Then start out by meditating for two minutes at a set time each day. As you begin to feel more comfortable and confident in your ability to stay focused, you can slowly start to add time to your meditation experience. When I was beginning my own practice, I started out meditating two minutes each afternoon. Because I found that short amount of time so do-able, I could never come up with an excuse not to meditate! Then I simply added one minute per day until I reached twenty minutes, which became my set time.

The goal is for you to leave your meditative state feeling relaxed and refreshed. If you find that you're becoming sleepy or are losing your concentration, then stick with a shorter time. Remember to feel free to experiment. I believe that even two minutes of meditation practice each day is better than none at all.

As an added bonus, research has proven that a regular meditation practice can lead to better sleep, stress reduction, improved mental health, lowered blood pressure and a host of other benefits!

Another option for strengthening your ability to be mindful is to focus on a chore, like washing the dishes or folding laundry. The key is to choose something and then practice directing your attention to it. If you find that your attention wanders, all you need to do is notice what is happening, and then gently bring your focus back to what you were originally concentrating on. You can also develop this skill by making a commitment to practice it with each meal, since you have that opportunity multiple times each day.

WITNESS CONSCIOUSNESS

This aspect of mindfulness refers to the capacity to notice your thoughts and feelings without becoming caught up in them. It is as though you are an outside observer objectively watching what is happening in your mind. You can access witness consciousness by paying attention to your thoughts and emotions as they arise – and then noticing as they dissipate and are replaced by new ones. In this way, witness consciousness will give you a broad perspective of yourself as you realize that there is more to you than just the thoughts and feelings that you experience. And most importantly, that you are **not** your thoughts and feelings! That is, there is a core self that exists beyond those sensations...

The sensation of being a curious, objective observer of your inner workings will allow you to recognize that you do not have to get completely consumed by what you are thinking or feeling. It demonstrates that there is a part of you that is of a more essential nature, and that what you are observing, as much as it might feel permanent in that moment, is actually transitory. Tapping into your witness consciousness also gives you the power to learn about the patterns of thinking that cause you pain. As you become familiar with your mental process, and discover when and where certain thought patterns occur, you can use your self-knowledge to short-circuit habitual, automatic responses that are unhelpful.

Again, using food as an example, you can use your witness consciousness to observe your mental and emotional states as you make a decision about what and how to eat. By paying attention to your emotions, what you're thinking and how your body feels, you could tell yourself, "I am aware that I'm angry and that I am thinking that what happened at work is unfair. I also notice that I'm craving cookies right now. I know that I am not hungry for food, but I still want to eat because I believe that eating those cookies will make me feel better." This kind of conversation with yourself will certainly be new and different if you are used to dealing with a distressing feeling by simply going for food without thinking about it.

As you learn to pay close attention to what you are feeling and the thoughts going through your head, you will be able to make important connections. In this case, you can clearly see that your desire to eat cookies is connected with feeling stressed. That knowledge buys you time, since you can step back and ask yourself, "Since I know that I want to eat those cookies because I am upset, not because I am hungry, is this a good choice for me? Is there some other way to deal with this stress that doesn't involve doing something I know I'll regret immediately afterwards?"

TIP: This kind of mental distance is especially helpful when you have a thought or feeling that begins with "I am ---." For example, you might think to yourself, "I am scared to get on that plane." Or, "I am stupid for making that mistake." This language is dangerous, because the verb "I am" refers to an enduring reality, and makes no allowance for the fact that your feelings and thoughts represent only one aspect of who you are, and temporarily at that. So rather than thinking "I am scared to get on the plane," you can tell yourself, "**I am having the feeling of** being scared…" Or if you notice that you're thinking to yourself, "I can't believe I just did that – I'm so stupid!", you can instead rephrase it as, "**I am having the thought** that I am stupid."

Although a bit awkward, this kind of phrasing has two advantages. First, it will remind you that instead of being permanent, these thoughts and feelings are actually transitory – they pass. Second, your witness consciousness allows you to recognize the inner workings of your thinking and feeling process. This in turn leads to empowerment, because once you understand that your thoughts are not facts but instead messages that you are giving yourself, then you can take a step back and decide exactly how seriously to take those messages and what to do about them. I'll talk more about how to do that later in the book in the chapter on how to overcome irrational thinking.

HOLDING THOUGHTS LIGHTLY

For this aspect of mindfulness, it's helpful to refer to the Buddhist concept of *nonattachment*, which refers to the idea that everything is temporary. We create suffering for ourselves when we believe that something is permanent and therefore become attached to it. Such clinging only leads to pain because nothing in life stays the same. People, places, things, pets, memories – all are temporary. That is, sooner or later either we or they pass out of our lives. Nothing is ever static – everything is either in a state of growth or decay.

This includes our inner dialogue as well. For example, we often become distressed when we focus on a particular thought (such as, "I can't believe I did that – I'm so embarrassed!"). We go over it endlessly in our mind, repeating it over and over. In psychology we refer to this as "*rumination.*" In its original meaning, rumination means that a cow is re-chewing something that has already been chewed slightly and swallowed. Now for an animal, that's a natural process that helps it digest food. For a person, however, not so good. After all, once we chew and swallow something, our body is supposed to process and eliminate it. But when it comes to worrying, we often keep thoughts swirling in our heads without letting them go. Dwelling continually on negative thoughts – as if we were a dog refusing to let its favorite bone go – often leads to suffering, which then awakens our addictive or compulsive nature.

By making a commitment to holding our thoughts lightly we remind ourselves that they are not actual, enduring facts. This type of mindfulness practice will help you avoid becoming entangled in your thinking. By committing to simply noticing the thoughts and images coming up for you in your mind, you will soon realize that they are part of a never-ending stream. Like clouds floating along in the sky, they come and then soon go.

Even the most distressing thoughts, such as "This is hopeless" or "I'll never be able to do this right" eventually dissipate and give way to new thoughts – something you'll soon notice if you let that process occur naturally. In that sense, ruminating on a thought keeps you trapped in a negative feedback loop. Or perhaps it is more accurate to say that rumination leads into a downward spiral, as the more time you spend chasing your tail in a mental circle, the more distressed you will become.

Consider the following Buddhist parable:

A senior monk and a junior monk were travelling together. At one point, they came to a river with a strong current. As the monks were preparing to cross the river, they saw a young and beautiful woman also attempting to cross. The young woman asked if they could help her.
The senior monk replied that he could and gently picked up the woman. Carrying her on his shoulder, they successfully crossed the river. The the monk let the woman down and bid her farewell. The junior monk seemed upset, but said nothing.

Both monks continued walking on their journey. Sometime later the senior monk noticed that his junior was particularly quiet and asked "Is something the matter? You seem upset."

The junior monk replied, "As monks, we are not permitted any contact with women, certainly not physical contact. How could you carry that woman on your shoulders?" The senior monk smiled and said, "That's interesting....I left the woman at the bank of the river a long time ago. You, however, seem to be still carrying her."

TIP #1: You can become skilled at this type of mindfulness through a certain type of meditation. This particular practice consists of sitting quietly in a space where you won't be disturbed. When you are settled, close your eyes and allow your mind to be open to all of the thoughts that pass through it. At the same time, permit your body to be open to all of the feelings that it experiences. Instead of focusing on a single thing, just let your thoughts arise naturally. The key is to let the thoughts come and go without attaching energy and attention to them. Don't dwell on them. Don't judge them. Simply be open to whatever arises. Notice what you are thinking. Observe what comes up. But then allow new thoughts and feelings to follow. Just observe what this experience is like.

TIP #2: If you find that your anxiety is interfering with your ability to let go of your thoughts, here is an idea that works for some people. Schedule thirty minutes per day that you will dedicate solely to worrying. When anxious thoughts come up outside of those thirty minutes, tell yourself that those thoughts can go away and wait for their scheduled time, during which you can ruminate on them all you want! I have found that those thoughts often will respond to your request...

ACCEPTANCE

This aspect of mindfulness is the acknowledgment of the things that are happening to us – without trying to analyze, resist, or change them. By practicing acceptance, we commit ourselves to be fully present with whatever we are feeling and experiencing. No clinging. No rejecting. One of the Buddha's major teachings is that by resisting or struggling with an uncomfortable experience, we actually increase our suffering. This is because when we ignore or disown our thoughts, emotions, and sensations, we are actually ignoring or disowning a part of ourselves. After all, if you are thinking or feeling something, then it is legitimate on some level. So the key is not to deny something you are thinking or feeling. Rather, the solution lays in what you do decide to do with those thoughts and feelings. Do you ruminate over them or let them take their natural course? Do you keep your focus on them or let them pass?

Acceptance consists of releasing our expectations about how we would like things to happen in our lives. Because the outcome is often out of our control, all we can do is be fully present in each moment. And of course try our best in each moment as well. But wishing something were different than how it is in that momement is like walking up to a brick wall and smacking your head against it. There is no way to win that fight with reality. Of course, how we respond to the present sets us up for the moments that follow. So that is important to keep in mind.

Certainly, it is true that we often wish the present moment were different than the way it actually is. For example, you might be driving somewhere and get suck in traffic. Yet all the cursing in the world isn't going to make the cars move more quickly. In that moment, you can avoid suffering and instead experience peace by taking a deep breath and accepting what is out of your control. Actually, you may find that the moment you accept that which you have been resisting, is the moment that your relationship to it changes – for the better.

TIP: The best way I know how to become clear about my control (or lack thereof) over reality is through **The Serenity Prayer**. The author of this prayer is thought to be the Protestant theologian Reinhold Niebuhr, who composed it in the early 1940s. Think of it as a guiding light when you have to make a decision about where to focus your energy.

**God grant me the serenity
to accept the things I cannot change;
the courage to change the things I can;
and the wisdom to know the difference.**

We can access that "wisdom to know the difference" by taking the time to ask ourselves what is truly possible or impossible in a given situation. And then, based on the answer, we can either take the appropriate action or make peace with what is. Both choices require the courage to feel discomfort. But that discomfort is temporary, as opposed to the permanent suffering we experience when we are mistaken about the power we do or don't have in our lives.

ACCEPTANCE AS NON-JUDGMENT

Acceptance also means acknowledging something without judging it. By going into our heads and labeling something as "good" or "bad" we prevent ourselves from experiencing it fully. Wishing something were different than it actually is, we cause ourselves frustration and distress. This of course can lead to engaging in an addictive or compulsive behavior, which is why this aspect of mindfulness is so important. Non-judgment is accepting something as it is, without overlaying our preference one way or another onto it. After all, when you fight with reality and focus on the way you wish things *would* or *could* be, you only create suffering. Now this doesn't necessarily mean that it is OK when bad things happen to you. As you will learn in later in this book, there are strategies you can use to make peace with reality without approving of it.

To practice this skill, simply notice the evaluations you make about yourself and others. When you are tempted to criticize or judge yourself, you must remember that you are doing the best you can. And when you evaluate others, it helps to do so with a sense of compassion, as it is impossible to know the real reasons behind other people's actions. This does not mean unconditional acceptance of behavior that harms others. Instead, this form of mindfulness asks you to consider that a person always makes the best choice they can, given their view of the world and the abilities they possess. A person's choice may be self-defeating, strange or hurtful, but for them it is the best choice at the time. The key is to acknowledge the positive intention of the other person's behavior.

In order to develop this skill, pay attention to how often you make judgments. What do you notice happens in your body when you judge or complain? Do you feel any tightness? What happens to your mood? What if you replaced your judgmental stance with a sense of detached curiosity? How might that make you feel?

As I mentioned above, when we wish something weren't the way it is, we are actually fighting with reality. And that is a fight we can never win. For example, if I forget to buy milk, I can berate myself for being stupid and forgetful. But that doesn't change the fact that the milk was forgotten. It is more helpful to recognize that I forgot to buy milk and then ask myself what I now need to do about it. In doing so, I now have created an opportunity to treat myself more gently. Even if I still have the judgmental thought, I can observe that I am having the thought, that I am doing the best I can in the moment, and then let it go. That's the beauty of being nonjudgmental; all the negative messages we're used to telling ourselves are suddenly cut off and the ensuing compassion creates the possibility of inner peace.

TIP: It is difficult to live without making judgments. Our preferences for how we'd like things to be or go fill our heads constantly. So don't be hard on yourself if you find it difficult to be judgment-free. Rather, I believe the benefit from this skill occurs if you simply observe a judgment when it arises in your mind, note that it is occurring, and then let the thought move away. Just notice and breathe. Notice that you actually have a choice when it comes to ruminating on the judgment. Another key is to remember that a judgment is not a fact. And a final suggestion is that when you find yourself making a judgment, you can ask yourself a simple question: "Is having this thought helpful?" Your answer will help you decide whether or not it is beneficial for you to focus on that line of thinking.

CHAPTER 3

Food and Eating: Practical Considerations

Let food be your medicine, and medicine be your food.

Hippocrates, the father of modern medicine

How you do anything is how you do everything.

Anonymous

A cornerstone of our health – and quality of life – is the relationship we have with food and eating. If you already have a good one feel free to skip this chapter. Otherwise, consider reading it through. There is a lot to be gained and it will make your journey of recovery all the easier. Especially because we truly are what we eat. Science demonstrates that what we put into our bodies has a huge impact on how we feel – physically, emotionally and mentally. And having the perfect amount of energy to get through the day is something you'd like to have, right?. Personally, I have learned that what I eat today will have a major impact on how I am going to feel for the rest of that day, as well as the next.

I don't want to mess around with that.

This is a type of power not to be ignored.

In addition, when things are spiraling out of control in our lives and we are feeling lost, often one of the few things we *can* control is what we put in our mouths...unless we have a dysfunctional connection with food and eating. Since it's such a major part of our everyday life, having a good relationship with food will make it easier for you to hold a steady course as you move forward on your journey toward a new sense of self. And make no mistake, this isn't about diets or dieting. Cookie-cutter methods don't work because each one of us is unique. Instead, the key is mindfulness plus intuition. You'll see what I mean as you make your way through this chapter...

THE *WHY* OF EATING

Ostensibly, we eat when we are hungry in order to provide energy and nutrients for our body. So what are some reasons we might eat when we are not hungry? Consider the following list:

- o Not listening to what our stomach is telling us (for example, we might keep eating even though we already feel full)

- o Confusing hunger with actually being thirsty

- o Being unable to achieve a feeling of satisfaction with what is being eaten, and so continuing to eat

- o Having a meal just because the clock says it's time to eat

- o Having a sense of obligation to finish what is on the plate

- Feeling any one of a number of emotions that bring on the urge to eat

- Feeling that the food tastes too good not to eat

- Feeling bored

- Feeling tired

- Being worried about offending someone if the food isn't eaten

- Being influenced by advertising and marketing

- Using food as a reward

- Eating in order to celebrate

- Using food as self-punishment

- Eating out of habit

- Eating food just because it is there

- Being attracted to a certain food because it brings back memories (smell, taste, texture)

- Using food to avoid pain

- Having a craving

- Using food in order to self-soothe

Journal Questions

What are some of the reasons you eat when you are not hungry?

What are the costs to you of eating when you are not hungry?

THE *WHEN* OF EATING

Nature operates on the rhythmic principle of ebb and flow, contraction and expansion. Each year has its seasonal cycle. Each day has its time of dark and light. Each moment you are breathing in and then breathing out. Everything in the universe is in rhythmic motion, right down to the pulsations of energy particles at the deepest quantum level. So it is with hunger and fullness. Taking food into your body (as well as refraining from doing so) is part of an eternal cycle that you will experience as long as you are alive.

Moving throughout the course of the day and evening, your body will naturally give you cues as to how hungry and how satisfied it is. The issue is, first, how aware are you of those messages? And second, how willing are you to respect them?

Simply stated, peace with food means listening to your body and eating when you are hungry. Peace with food means finishing your meal when you are no longer hungry, but instead feel satisfied (*before* you feel the fullness in your belly). Peace with food means honoring the role of food in your life as a gift of nurturance, and not using food as a way to get other needs met.

So – How will you know when you are truly hungry? How will you know when you are really satisfied and can stop eating? And what if you feel lost because you are unfamiliar with these sensations? It is time to re-learn those natural feelings of hunger and satisfaction. This can be done by paying close attention to what you are experiencing, both physically and mentally. It is vital that you listen to the intuitive wisdom of your body, as it knows exactly when it needs food and when it has had enough.

Take a moment to study the chart on the next page. It runs from starving to feeling uncomfortably stuffed. "The Hunger Scale" is a tool will give you an simple, convenient way to check in with yourself as you begin to pay attention to your body's need for food. Take a moment to familiarize yourself with it.

THE HUNGER SCALE

Starving
- You are physically ill, feeling light-headed and exhausted, with almost no energy.

Ravenous
- You are irritable and unable to concentrate; your stomach is empty and you crave food.

Very Hungry
- You hear your stomach rumbling and gurgling.

Hungry
- You notice that your energy level is low; the idea of eating food is attractive.

Slightly hungry
- You are beginning to feel hunger pangs; you are not yet compelled to eat but are thinking about your next meal.

Satisfied
- You feel perfectly comfortable and energized, and notice that you cannot feel the food in your stomach; you feel neither hungry nor full.

Mildly full
- You notice a slight sense of pressure in your stomach.

Full
- You can feel the heaviness of the food you've just eaten in your stomach; you need to loosen your clothes.

Uncomfortably full
- You are bloated and tired. You feel heavy and need to lie down.

Stuffed
- You are miserable, feeling sick to your stomach. The thought of food disgusts you.

From now on, when you are making a choice about what to eat for a meal or a snack, I would like you to take a deep breath and then ask yourself:

1. Where am I on the hunger scale? Am I *physically* hungry?
2. Do I want to eat in order to change the way I am feeling?
3. Do I actually want what I am gravitating towards?
4. Will I feel deprived if I don't eat it?
5. Will my choice be satisfying?
6. How does my choice fit into my chosen way of eating?
7. Is this food choice worthy of going into my body?
8. Does my choice taste good?
9. Will I feel guilty if I eat this?

For a simpler alternative, before you eat something simply close your eyes and project yourself into the future. You've been down this path thousands of times already – intuitively you already know how eating certain foods (and particular quantities of those foods) will make you feel afterwards. But now I would like you to deliberately consider the consequences of your action in order to see if it will really be worth it. So give yourself the following message:

"Let me imagine how I will feel after I have eaten what I am about to eat...Am I OK with the consequences?"

Finally, if you are aware that you are truly hungry for food, here are two good questions to ask yourself that your intuition will always be able to answer:

1. Is the food that I have chosen nourishing for my body? What nutrients does it actually provide for me?

2. If eating this particular food isn't in my best interest, then what foods would best nourish me at this time?

As you begin to regularly tune into your body during the day, and as you eat your meals, you will soon become quite familiar with The Hunger Scale. With the passage of time and experience, you will learn to quickly recognize where you are on the scale and then how to respond.

THE *HOW* OF EATING

Our personal histories often influence how we approach food and eating. Understanding your past will allow you to see how you developed your current relationship with food. It is vital to explore these connections so that you can recognize and then break old patterns that no longer serve you.

Please complete the following in your journal:

My favorite childhood foods were:

Typical family breakfasts took place in the following location:

Typical family dinners took place in the following location:

True or False: I looked forward to family meals. Why? Why not?

A typical family meal felt:

The things that we often talked about during meals were:

The rules in my family surrounding eating and meals consisted of:

Growing up, the main lessons I learned about making and eating food were:

My two most positive childhood memories regarding food are:

My two most disturbing childhood memories regarding food are:

Words that characterize my mother's relationship with food and cooking are:

Words that characterize my father's relationship with food and cooking are:

Some things I learned as a child or teenager about food and eating that are still part of my life today are:

Some messages about my body that I learned from my family were:

I first began to manipulate my eating habits and hunger when:

The thing that happened that led me to that change was:

Some examples of the different ways I have manipulated my eating habits and hunger are:

The consequences of doing so have been:

Now please answer the following questions about your current eating situation:

How do you plan your weekly menu? Are your meals well thought-out in advance?

Do you eat at the same times each day?

What is breakfast like for you? Is it rushed? Leisurely?

How are your dinners structured? Do you look forward to them?

What would you have to give up in order to spend more time and energy planning, preparing, and eating your meals? Why might it be worth it?

How willing are you to consider some new ways to plan, prepare and eat your meals? If you are not totally willing, what would have to change for you to increase your motivation?

The next sections in this chapter will provide a framework of each of your meals. Knowing when (and how) to start and stop eating will be essential to the development of a positive relationship with food.

BEGINNING YOUR MEAL

Consider the rhythm of your life. We all need consistent pacing in our lives, especially with meal times. This is because you can't properly digest food if you are stressed, rushing or distracted. The physiological consequences of stress greatly influence the amount of time food stays in your stomach, as well as how you physically feel it in there. So please consider giving yourself more time to eat. See if you can create an inviting, pleasant environment in which you would enjoy spending time. It is especially important to eat sitting down, using correct posture and not slouching, as that also affects the digestive process.

Of course, you have decided to eat in the first place because you are truly hungry for some food. That is why **The Hunger Scale** is so important. As babies and young children, we are naturally in tune with what our bodies need. But as we grow older we lose the ability to accurately gauge that sense of physical hunger. Instead, we find ourselves eating for all sorts of other reasons (as detailed in the first part of this chapter). Therefore, one of your major goals is to begin to reacquaint yourself with that feeling of true physical hunger. This means taking the time to notice the sensations you feel *below* your neck. Pay attention to your stomach and your energy level. Physical hunger does not equal the feeling of craving something to eat. Rather, it comes on gradually, without a sense of compulsion. Typically people begin to feel hungry 3-5 hours after their last meal. This means that you will feel the desire to eat in your stomach, not in your heart.

Of course, you don't want to wait until you reach the "starving" or "ravenous" zones on The Hunger Scale, since those often lead to binge eating. For some people getting too physically hungry can lead to irritability, fatigue, headaches, an inability to concentrate, or even dizziness. In addition, feeling your stomach growling and rumbling is also a sign that you have waited too long to eat. Monitoring your physical hunger so that you do not reach those levels of physical discomfort is a vital skill that you must learn. The key is noticing the message your stomach is telling you, and then acting on it instead of ignoring it. That is why learning the skill of mindfulness is so important: being able to pay careful attention to your body and feelings will allow you to be able to differentiate between physical and emotional hunger.

DURING YOUR MEAL

Now let's imagine that you have decided that you are physically hungry. Think about what you might experience if you were able to slow yourself down, choosing your food with deliberation and preparing it with care. What if you took some time to appreciate your food's color, texture, and aroma? As you chewed your food thoroughly and attentively, you might discover that as its texture changes with each chew, so does its flavor. At the same time, it is helpful to be conscious of how you are breathing while you eat. A regular, measured flow of oxygen in and carbon dioxide out helps your digestive system do its job properly and with ease. Distracted eating actually leads to less nutrient absorption.

Also, typically the more distracted a person is, the more he or she will consume. What about you? Do you tend to watch television or read during your meal? Do you find that when you eat you are disconnected from your food and are just going through the motions?

Please notice what it feels like to pay attention to what you are eating. See if you can give yourself permission to savor your food. It is helpful if you put down your fork or spoon in-between bites, picking it up again once you've completely chewed your current mouthful of food. Doing so will also aid you in determining when to stop eating (more about that shortly).

After each bite, you can ask yourself:

- How does it feel to eat this food?
- How is this food affecting me?
- Is there a connection between what I just ate and how I feel now?
- What am I noticing that changes with each bite of food?

FINISHING YOUR MEAL

One of the most important things you can do is to stop eating *before* you feel full. This will take courage and a strong belief in yourself because it will likely be a new – and very unfamiliar – way of eating for you. The key is to understand that there will be a point during your meal when you will feel neither hungry nor full. Your goal is to notice when you have more energy than you did when you first sat down to eat. In order to locate that point, simply slow down and pay attention to your energy level as you eat; notice how your stomach feels during your meal. Ideally, you should stop eating before you feel anything in your stomach.

Unfortunately, by the time you feel the food settling into your stomach, it is too late. Instead, you should be feeling that what you just ate has provided you with a sense of well-being and comfort. Therefore, the point at which you should stop eating is when you are no longer hungry but energized instead. Be sure to avoid being guided by your head (that is, expectations, judgments, thoughts). Instead, let the feelings in your body tell you exactly how much to eat and when to stop.

An easy way to check in with yourself after you have been eating awhile is to ask the following questions:

- "How am I feeling?"
- "How is my energy level?"
- "Am I noticing my stomach?"
- "Am I beginning to feel heaviness in my stomach?"

If you follow this method, you will know **exactly** when to end your meal. It might take some time to learn how to eat this way because it seems strange right now, but once you do you'll never have to weigh food or count calories again!

"THE CLEAN PLATE CLUB"

In the beginning, as you practice this new way of eating, you will discover that it will be difficult to judge how much food to serve yourself. Odds are you will be eating less than you are used to, but you'll still be giving yourself the same portions as before. This means there will be times when you will have to leave some food over on your plate. So despite everything your parents told you about starving children in third world countries, you will have to learn how to be comfortable not finishing what is in front of you. My thinking is, if you eat it because you don't want to "waste" it, then you'll just carry the extra weight with you as opposed to dumping it in the garbage. Either way, the food is wasted.

Of course, I would certainly advise you to take precautions against wasting food. And you can always save your leftovers for later. However, it is important to get used to not finishing everything on your plate, too, since it will take some time to learn how to accurately judge how much food is best for you to consume at one sitting. One solution is to put less on your plate to begin with. When serving yourself food, be mindful of how much food you're taking, and always give yourself less rather than more. After all, you can always serve yourself extra if you discover you are still hungry!

The challenge for you is that other people will become confused or even upset when they see you eating smaller portions or leaving over some of your meal. People often feel good when they can offer food to others, especially guests. It will take a strong belief in yourself to follow your own course and refuse to be swayed by others' expectations of you (due to their own food and eating issues).

AFTER THE MEAL

Once you've finished eating, it is preferable to wait five minutes before you engage in another activity. This gives your digestive system even more time to do its job effectively before blood and oxygen get re-directed to someplace else in your body.

After eating, pay attention to how you feel. This information is invaluable, since it will give you feedback about what is right and not so right for your body and its well-being. Asking yourself the following questions can be quite useful. One of the best ways to record this information is by keeping a food diary:

- o Time of day and location
- o What you ate
- o Does your body react to the food in a particular way?
- o Does the food enhance or drain your energy?
- o How is your mood after the meal?
- o How did you feel one hour after eating?
- o How did you feel the next morning?
- o Did you notice any physical symptoms after the meal (such as burping, gas or cramps)?
- o Did you notice any physical symptoms the following day (for example, skin breaking out)?
- o What does your intuition tell you about whether this food is right for you or not?

THE *WHAT* OF EATING

Eating is the most intimate thing a person can do...the food you eat actually becomes a part of you! Plus, anything you ingest will create various chemical reactions within your body. This means that each thing you eat will have an effect on you, physically, emotionally and mentally. Your goal is to pay attention to how different foods affect you, and then choose accordingly. As you learn more about how certain foods make you feel, you'll naturally gravitate towards those that make you feel good and give you positive energy and avoid what makes you feel bad.

As I mentioned above, a food diary is a great way to keep track of how particular foods and meals affect your physical and mental states of being. This means what you eat is not going to be based on specific dietary guidelines or a restrictive regimen. Rather, it is based on noticing how you feel after you've eaten: immediately following a meal, the hours afterwards, and even the next day. By keeping a food diary, you will be able to easily spot patterns so that you can modify what and how you eat. Therefore, no food is off-limits – unless **you** want it to be.

Personally, the way I decide whether or not to eat something is to ask myself, "Is this food clogging or cleansing?" Intuitively, I know the answer immediately. And so will you! The key is to honor the choices that you know will truly serve your best interests.

Ideally, your diet should be based on intuitive eating: Nothing is off-limits. When and how you eat is more important than what you eat. *However*, since knowledge is power, you might be interested in considering the following information:

➢ Protein and high fiber foods are very satisfying nutrients (both empty out of the stomach slowly). Simple sugars are least satisfying because they empty from the stomach very quickly. Interestingly, fat is very satisfying because it empties from the stomach most slowly. The problem, however, is that we tend to keep eating fat past satiation….

➢ Pay attention to your caffeine intake – it is a powerful drug.

➢ Notice your white sugar intake – it is also a powerful drug and causes inflammation.

➢ Consider your consumption of processed foods – they contain many synthetic chemicals that can have profound effects both on your physical as well as emotional/mental health.

➢ Be curious about food labels, so you can be informed about what you are putting into your body. If you can't pronounce an ingredient, you might want to think twice about consuming it.

➢ It is easier to digest warm foods compared to cold foods, especially in the morning.

➢ It is also easier to digest cooked or steamed foods than raw foods.

➢ We are often allergic to the foods which we crave…seems paradoxical but it's worth exploring.

- Pay attention to your water intake. When you feel hungry, it is usually because you are thirsty! Water is important because it:
    - Maintains blood pressure and flow
    - Digests the food you eat
    - Transports nutrients throughout your body
    - Eliminates waste products from your body
    - Decreases constipation
    - Protects and lubricates your organs and tissues
    - Regulates and maintains your body temperature
    - Metabolizes fat
    - Gives a feeling of fullness

- Consider your breakfast foods and how you eat them.

    - First of all, have breakfast! You've been sleeping all night and it's time to break your fast – this is a vital meal that will give you energy for the rest of the morning. Unless of course you're not hungry in the morning – then don't.
    - Notice how you are balancing protein, carbohydrates and fats. A balanced combination of all three ensures a steady supply of energy throughout the morning.
    - See if you can detect a difference in how you feel after eating a warm meal at breakfast, such as oatmeal, versus a cold one, such as cereal with milk.
    - Consider your pace of eating breakfast – are you rushing or eating in your car? Or are you able to relax while you eat?
    - Experiment with drinking water (at room-temperature) first thing in the morning at least a half hour before you eat. See how this helps to regulate your bowel movements and increase your energy.

- Pay attention to those foods that hold your blood sugar steady and don't cause you to feel lethargic after an initial burst of energy.

- Intermittent fasting is when you eat all of your meals within an eight or six hour window of time. Typically this means that you skip either breakfast or dinner. For some people, this pattern of eating leads to increased energy and weight loss.

***

There is an old saying: "As above, so below." I believe that it will be difficult for you to heal from your addiction or compulsive behavior if you do not have a healthy relationship with food and eating. Eating a lousy diet will throw your balance off and become a distraction from the work that's necessary for your journey forward. Finding the foods that make you feel good – physically, mentally and emotionally – will give you the energy you need to create the strong foundation on which your recovery will be based.

CHAPTER 4

Accessing Authentic Values

Your soul suffers if you live superficially.

Albert Schweitzer

And the day came when the risk it took to remain tight inside the bud was more than the risk it took to blossom.

Anais Nin

Your work is to discover your world and then with all your heart give yourself to it.

the Buddha

It takes courage to grow up and become who you really are.

e.e. cummings

To be at peace with ourselves, we need to know ourselves.

Caitlin Matthews

By creating a connection with your deepest values, you will strengthen your foundation as you move forward with your recovery. Being clear and comfortable about who you are and what you stand for will allow you to develop the motivation and commitment necessary for creating positive changes in your life. Most importantly, being aligned with your true values automatically gives you the ability to make **the** right choice when you are faced with a decision about **anything**. The mindfulness skills you have learned will allow you to connect with your deepest values in the present moment, and from there you will instantly know how to proceed. Your decision-making process will be effortless – and you won't feel regret with the choices you've made.

WHAT EXACTLY ARE VALUES?

Values are personal beliefs about what is good and bad, or right and wrong. They are also ideas about what is important to us in life. We typically want more of what we value in our lives and less of what we do not. Our values point us in particular directions and steer us away from others. Some of the values we hold are situational, and apply to specific times, contexts, or people. Other values are much more connected to who we are at our core and transcend any specific situation. They guide us across all the domains of our lives. These core values determine the people and opportunities we seek out, and the ones we avoid. They shape the goals we set in life, and then motivate us to move toward those goals. Ultimately, they are the standards we use to evaluate our own actions and the actions of others.

Core values lead to clear intentions, which then point the way to committed actions. Think about it: People who are the same way on the inside as they are on the outside are truly aligned. There is no dissonance between what they feel and how they act. They have **integrity,** which comes from the Latin word *integer*, meaning "one."

When we are connected to values that deeply resonate with us, change comes naturally. That is, when our values are guiding us, our decision-making process becomes effortless. There simply isn't a question of what to do, since following our values makes it immediately clear which course to follow. This might be challenging, since sometimes we have to spend time around people whose values are in conflict with our own. But the knowledge that your actions are aligned with what you truly believe can be its own source of strength.

Here are some examples of values:

Nature	Money	Work	Leisure
Music	Fun	Independence	Volunteering
Animals	Family	Learning	Discipline
Travel	Adventure	Balance	Community
Curiosity	Justice	Recognition	Wisdom
Fairness	Pleasure	Self-growth	Toughness
Spirituality	Risk-taking	Gratitude	Friendship
Honesty	Responsibility	Popularity	Security
Status	Diversity	Faith	Creativity
Non-conformity	Persistence	Children	Optimism
Education	Loyalty	Courtesy	Health

WHERE DO VALUES COME FROM?

Values aren't something we are born with. Instead, we learn them as we grow up. Value systems are influenced by our childhood environment. Parents, peers, school, religious institutions, and the media all send us messages about what is good and bad, acceptable and unacceptable about ourselves and the world around us. As children we are sponges and soak everything up. However, it is important to realize that because we have learned our values, we can also unlearn them if we eventually discover that they do not serve our best interests.

Where did *your* values come from? The following journal questions will help you understand how your value system was created. You can answer these questions all in one sitting or spread them out over a period of several days. It is important that you take your time with them and give yourself support if necessary, since they might bring up some powerful memories.

(Note: I use the words "mother" and "father" in the questions below; if you were raised by a grandparent or some other caretaker, please substitute accordingly).

Write five adjectives to describe what it was like to grow up in your home.

Who were the main people in your home environment? Please describe what your relationship was like with each one.

Which adjectives would best describe your mother?

How did you get along with your mother when you were a child?

What are five things you learned from your mother (positive or negative)?

Which adjectives would best describe your father?

What kind of relationship did you have with your father when you were a child?

What were five things you learned from your father (positive or negative)?

Were your relationships with your mother and father similar? Different? How so?

What kinds of things did you do together as a family when you were a child?

When you were a child, did your mother and/or father ever reject you? Can you remember any specific examples? How did you feel when you were rejected? How did you respond?

When you were a child, how did your care-takers discipline you? Were there ever any punishments that made a strong impression on you? Were there any that you can still vividly remember?

What kinds of messages did you receive about yourself from your father and mother? What did you learn about your role in life from your parents? Do you feel those messages influenced your life? If so, how?

When you were a child, did anybody close to you (friend or relative) pass away? Do you remember your experience of that time? Do you remember if you were able to grieve? And if so, how you grieved? Did you receive assistance from anybody in understanding and processing that death?

As a child, were there people in your life who you could count on for support besides your parents? What were those relationships like?

During childhood, did you have any coping mechanisms that helped you feel safe when you were threatened, or made you feel better when you were sad, anxious or upset? Are any of these coping mechanisms still present in your life as an adult? Do they still work? Are there any negative side effects?

Was your family religious? Were there certain ideas and rules about life that you learned from your religious tradition?

Were certain expectations communicated to you, either implicitly or explicitly, about how you were supposed to behave or be? What about career goals? Did you ever experience judgment or disapproval from your parents if you expressed interest in a certain hobby or career?

Based on the answers to the above questions, what do you now know about how your concept of yourself – and the world around you – was created? Do you believe that the experiences you had growing up may have influenced the decisions you made later in life? Have you discovered any evidence that how you think and feel about yourself and the world today as an adult might be connected to your childhood experiences?

It is important that you understand that you weren't born knowing good from bad. You learned those standards while growing up by receiving messages from the people and institutions in your life. It can be quite empowering to recognize that those standards – those values – were learned. Which means that you can adjust them if necessary.

Now it is time to focus on your current values. Think back to the definition of "values" from above. These are ways of being that are important to you, that resonate with your soul. These are the things that are important to you in how you live your life. Examples such as family, achievement, adventure, honesty, assertivenss, city life or solitude. Other values could be: never quitting, always being perfect, being there for others, or not showing anger. As you can see, there is a wide range of possibilities!

You can begin to articulate your own values in the following way. First, please number 1-15 on a blank sheet of paper in your journal. On the top of the page, write the heading, "**I value:**" Now fill in as many of the 15 spaces as you are able. It doesn't matter what you write or how you write it, just as long as it is recognizable as a "value."

When you are done, copy down your answers onto a separate piece of paper, but now also include **why** each is important to you.

After you have finished, take a break for at least an hour (a day is better). When you feel refreshed, come back to your list of values. Take some time to look them over. Notice how you feel in your gut when you read what you have written. You may end up discarding some of your current values because you can now recognize that they don't serve your best interests. Others you may decide to keep. The following part of this exercise will assist you in making those decisions. Once again, take your time with this. It is perfectly fine to break it up over several days or over the course of a week.

For each of the values that you have listed, please read and then think about the following statements. Use your answers to help you determine whether to keep or discard each of your values.

- I have chosen this value consciously and deliberately
- I know how and why this value became important to me
- This is a core part of who I am
- Without this value I would be a different person
- My life is aligned around this value
- My future goals are connected to this value
- This value resonates deeply within me
- This value empowers me
- This value can cause me to feel badly about myself
- This value has led to situations which I later regreted
- I always notice this value in other people
- I very much want to have this value in my life
- When this value is threatened, I feel emotional pain
- I feel satisfied when I am actively expressing this value in my life
- Every day, I am able to express this value in some manner
- I have made sacrifices for the sake of this value
- I am attracted to people and situations that also have this value

You might notice that some of your values bring you peace or fulfillment. Others may cause you suffering or conflict. It's good that you are noticing; I want you to become conscious of how your values have impacted – and continue to impact – the quality of your life.

This is a powerful time of transition. You have the chance now, as an adult, to consciously create a value system that will serve your higher good. Therefore it is natural that you will have some values that you know you would like to keep, while there are others that you would like to release. It is vital to remember that this process will bring about a change in you as a person. As you readjust your value system, you are becoming a different person than you were before. This may create anxiety, because you are entering new territory. Therefore, it may be helpful for you to think about how to mourn the values that you are leaving behind. After all, they were part of your life for a long time.

SAYING "GOODBYE" TO A VALUE

The most important thing to remember when you release a value that no longer serves you is that you learned it from someone or somewhere else – you weren't born with it. Let's take perfeccionism as an example. At the time you learned it, the idea that you had to do things "perfectly" seemed like a necessary fact of life. Force may have been involved, or perhaps it was appealing on some other level, like gaining approval from your parents. But if you're honest, you'll realize that perfeccionism causes nothing but suffering; after all, nothing and no one is perfect. So once you recognize that you have the power to let a value go, you can imagine that, like a snake, you are shedding skin that you have outgrown. And that's OK. You can silently wish that value a "good-bye" and remind yourself that it doesn't have to guide your decisions anymore. You now know that there are other, more empowering ways to lead your life. (a nice replacement for perfeccionism is "being OK with good enough")

Because this is an in-between, transitional, time for you, it is especially important to recognize and honor this process of releasing and becoming. By making peace with what was formerly important to you, and understanding why it is in your best interests to leave certain values behind, you will clear the path for new growth as you move forward. The challenge you have is being willing to trust your intuition as it guides you to a way of grieving for the values you are leaving behind. Those values were once a very deep part of you. And as the author William Bridges notes, "You have to make an ending before you make a beginning." He further writes:

Transition does not require that you reject or deny the importance of your old life, just that you let go of it. Far from rejecting it, you are likely to do better with the ending if you honor the old life for all that it did for you. It got you this far. It brought you everything you have. But now – although it may be some time before you are comfortable actually doing so – it is time for you to let go of it. Your old life is over. No matter how much you would like to continue it or rescue it or fix it, it's time to let it go.

When you feel ready, it will be time to continue your search for other empowering values to add to the ones you already have. The journal questions below will give you a chance to search out and reconnect with important parts of yourself that perhaps have been buried or denied since childhood. Now is the time to get in touch with what is truly important to you, what makes you feel alive, having a life worth living.

As you consciously create a value-system based on your own (not somebody else's) standards, you will set in place a way of looking at the world – and being in it – which will feel "right" to you. It will feel honest. You will feel comfortable owning it. When you can stand in the certainty of who are as a person, knowing in your bones what you stand for and what you believe in, then you will be able to access the motivation and commitment to follow a path of positive change, especially when it comes to food and eating.

Journal questions

By answering the following questions, you will gain important insights about yourself that perhaps you have forgotten or are unconscious of. This information will allow you to make additions to your list of core values, those things and ways of being that are truly important to you.

Just to let you know upfront, the large number of questions you'll be answering might make you feel you've entered a values-generating boot camp! So be easy on yourself and take your time. There is no rush. By giving each question the consideration it deserves, you will be presenting yourself with a powerful gift.

Think back to when you were a child. What did you want to be when you grew up? What was it about your choice(s) that made you feel excited?

When you were young, did you have one or more favorite television shows? What were they? What was it about them that made an impression on you?

Growing up, did you have a favorite book? What was it about that book that resonated with you?

What was your favorite movie as a child? Why? What about now, as an adult?

How did you sprend your free time as a child? As a teen?

Describe a time when you felt that you were truly alive.

What brings tears to your eyes?

If time and money were not an issue, what would you do with your life? What would your days look like?

Happiness is (use 7 words):

What would you like to do someday?

Describe a time in your life when you felt that you were doing what you were born to do.

List ten wishes.

I love: (list 10 nouns/10 verbs)

What is your wildest dream?

What would make your life perfect?

Ideally, where would you like to be in your life five years from now?

What matters to you?

Who would you like to serve in your life? To whom would you like to make a difference?

Think of three people (past or present) who you respect and admire. For each of these people, list three qualities which resonate with you.

What are you tolerating in your life?

Which people/places/things drain you of energy?

Which people/places/things give you energy?

Imagine you are an old person, looking back on your life.

      o About what did you worry way too much?
      o What do you wish you had done less of? More of?

Imagine that you are on your death bed. You have lived a long life. Answer the following question: "What was it that made your life worth living?"

What will allow you to die without regrets?

What would you like your legacy to be?

What would the epitaph on your gravestone say?

You are on your deathbed. What were the three most important lessons you learned in your life?

In the end, what did you stand for?

***

So at this point, what have you discovered about who you "really" are? What do you now know is **truly** important to you? Go back to the original list you made of your core values. What would you add or subtract? What are the factors you would like to have guiding the decisions you make in life? Remember, each decision that you make in life is either in or out of alignment with your core values.

MISSION STATEMENT EXERCISE

Now I would like you to create what is commonly known as a "mission statement." This is a piece of writing in which you summarize your values and outline what you feel your purpose in life is. It can also include your aspirations and what you would like to achieve in the future. Your wording, the tone, and the length of your mission statement are all up to you. There certainly are plenty of possibilities. Just make sure that what you write resonates deeply within you!

Think of your mission statement as your "personal constitution" or philosophy of life. Creating a personal mission statement provides you with clarity because it defines in writing who you are and how you have decided to live your life. It also succinctly summarizes what is important to you and is an easily accessed reminder of your priorities.

Your mission statement should uplift you, so please make it a part of your life. You can keep it in your journal or incorporate it into a piece of art or collage. You could also make a small version of it and keep it in your purse or wallet. You could frame it or just tape it to your wall. Or you could stick it on your refrigerator or bathroom mirror. It doesn't matter – just keep it available for inspiration. Since it captures the essence of who you are and who you want to be, make sure you allow it to empower you by having it handy! As the days, weeks and months pass, you will internalize your mission statement, so physical copies won't be as necessary. But remember – as your life changes, it is perfectly fine to go back and change your mission statement. It is not set in stone. So let it evolve as you do!

To give you a sense of the possibilities, I have provided some examples of mission statements.

Example #1:

My one-sentence mission: To live a balanced life in which I look out for the well-being of others while also honoring my own needs.

My detailed personal mission:

Words that describe me: compassionate, loving, spiritual, balanced, curious, adventure-seeking, persistent, dreamer, educator, advocate, self-aware, father, husband.

I am compassionate. I care about others and want to serve their best-interests. I always want to be sure that I can be of service to the best of my abilities.

I am spiritual. I have a daily spiritual practice that connects me to my higher power. This gives me strength.

I am balanced. I always seek to have balance in my life, making sure that no one area in my life overpowers the rest.

I am curious. I love to learn and will never stop being a student.

I am adventurous. I love to travel and will always look for opportunities to have new experiences.

I am a husband and father. I am dedicated to my family. Every decision I make must take into account the fact that I want to be there for my family.

Example #2:

"Slow down. Simplify. Be kind." (Naomi Judd)

Example #3:

"To be a teacher. And to be known for inspiring my students to be more than they thought they could be." (Oprah Winfrey)

Example #4:

"To inspire, lift and provide tools for change and growth of individuals and organizations throughout the world to significantly increase their performance capability in order to achieve worthwhile purposes through understanding and living principle-centered leadership." (Stephen Covey)

Example #5:

"To live each day with courage, compassion, and curiosity; to be come a better version of myself each day, and to inspire others in my path to do the same." (Kara Benz)

Example #6:

"Let the first act of every morning be to make the following resolve for the day:
I shall not fear anyone on earth.
I shall fear only God.
I shall not bear ill toward anyone.
I shall not submit to injustice from anyone.
I shall conquer untruth by truth.
And in resisting untruth, I shall put up with all suffering"
(Mahatma Gandhi)

Here is one of my favorite mission statements, from the journalist Erma Bombeck. Note the creative way she used to express her values:

"If I had my life to live over, I would have talked less and listened more. I would have invited friends over to dinner even if the carpet was stained and the sofa faded. I would have eaten the popcorn in the 'good' living room and worried much less about the dirt when someone wanted to light a fire in the fireplace. I would have taken the time to listen to my grandfather ramble about his youth. I would never have insisted the car windows be rolled up on a summer day because my hair had just been teased and sprayed. I would have burned the pink candle sculpted like a rose before it melted in storage. I would have sat on the lawn with my children and not worried about grass stains. I would have cried and laughed less while watching television - and more while watching life. I would have shared more of the responsibility carried by my husband. I would have gone to bed when I was sick instead of pretending the earth would go into a holding pattern if I weren't there for the day. I would never have bought anything just because it was practical, wouldn't show soil or was guaranteed to last a lifetime. Instead of wishing away nine months of pregnancy, I'd have cherished every moment and realized that the wonderment growing inside me was the only chance in life to assist God in a miracle. When my kids kissed me impetuously, I would never have said, "Later. Now go get washed up for dinner." There would have been more "I love you's"... More "I'm sorrys" ... But mostly, given another shot at life, I would seize every minute... look at it and really see it ... live it...and never give it back."

Now it's your turn.

THE POWER QUESTIONS

(HOW TO MAKE THE RIGHT CHOICE EVERY TIME)

Once you have completed your mission statement, you should be clear about the guiding principles of your life. From this point forward, when you are faced with a decision, asking yourself the following values-based questions beforehand will point you in the right direction.

1. Will my decision move me down a path I have defined as fulfilling or will it keep me stuck in the past?
2. Will my decision bring me satisfaction in the long-run or will it produce instant gratification – followed by remorse?
3. Is my decision congruent with my core values or am I doing this to make another person happy?
4. Is my decision based on love or fear?
5. Will my decision give me energy or will it deplete my life force?
6. Will my decision give me an opportunity to grow or will it give me an excuse to rehash old patterns?
7. Will my decision empower me or will it cause me to lose personal power?
8. Is this decision a way for me to be kind to myself or is it a way for me to hurt myself?

To boil it down, each time you have a decision to make about anything, simply ask yourself:

"Will what I choose bring me closer to what is truly important to me or

will it separate me?"

CHAPTER 5

Cultivating Self-Compassion

I do not trust people who don't love themselves and yet tell me, 'I love you.' There is an African saying which is: Be careful when a naked person offers you a shirt.

Maya Angelou

The feeling of being valuable – I am a valuable person – is essential to mental health and a cornerstone of self-discipline. It is the direct product of parental love...When one considers oneself valuable one will take care of oneself in all ways that are necessary.

M. Scott Peck

You can search throughout the entire universe for someone who is more deserving of your love and affection than you are yourself, and that person is not to be found anywhere. You yourself, as much as anybody in the entire universe, deserve your love and affection.

the Buddha

Be yourself. Everyone else is taken.

Oscar Wilde

So now you know exactly what you stand for and why. But what about liking yourself?

I believe that in order to create lasting, positive change we must first fully accept ourselves as we are. We also have to be willing to accept *where* we are in life. Self-rejection does not support growth. If you like yourself, you will treat yourself kindly. If you believe you have worth, you will not deliberately hurt yourself.

It is our responsibility to derive our self-worth from within, not from other people's opinions of us. It becomes our obligation to provide ourselves with nurturance, affection, and recognition, instead of expecting those things from other people.

This section provides an opportunity for you to think about what prevents you from being kind to yourself. In the last chapter you learned about your authentic self and what you stand for. Now it is time to explore topics such as:

- Self-nurturance
- Your needs and how to get them met
- Developing self-forgiveness
- The importance of gratitude

My hope is that by the end of this chapter, you will feel really, *really* good about yourself. And so your relationship with yourself – how you treat yourself – will naturally change. And this in turn will impact the place of your addiction or compulsive behavior in your life.

The key to positive change is making peace with yourself and believing that you are worthy of unconditional love. Learning to love yourself without limits will provide you with a core sense of self-worth that nobody can take away from you. But, as Julia Cameron notes, it is only when we truly believe that we are "precious objects" that we will be kind to ourselves.

The success of your recovery journey depends on you reaching a point where you feel comfortable treating yourself with compassion. I define self-compassion as a feeling of protective fondness. It means releasing harsh self-judgment. It means recognizing and honoring your inherent worth. It especially means that you are willing to address your own pain in a nurturing, understanding manner.

A CAVEAT ABOUT "SELF-ESTEEM"

I would like to talk a bit about "self-esteem," since it so often is included in discussions about feeling good about ourselves. The word "esteem" can be defined as "respect and admiration". Significantly, however, it is not something that you're automatically born with. Rather, it is something you have to "build" or work at maintaining.

So how might you build self-esteem? Typically, you do it by strengthening your ego in two ways. First, by having other people validate you ("I feel good about myself because my father said I'm a good artist"). Second, by comparing yourself favorably to others ("I feel good about myself because I won the race").

This leads to the idea that you can "create" self-esteem by achieving goals and being recognized by others as "special." Of course, the flip side to this is that you can also lose your self-esteem if you make a mistake or fail at something. For example, when somebody else gives you positive feedback about something, you feel good about yourself. And when somebody says something negative to or about you, then you will feel bad.

The result is that when you look outside of yourself for self-worth and self-definition, you give your power away to people who do not necessarily have your best interests in mind. This external dependence on other people's approval actually makes you powerless – and insecure.

Accordingly, self-esteem ebbs and flows depending on how people respond to you based on your actions; it is out of your control. On the other hand, your sense of *self-worth* is something that is constant because it is based on your inner "being." No outside source can diminish it because it is constant, no matter what happens outside of you.

But how do we connect with self-compassion and our inherent self-worth? How do we reach a point where we really believe that, no matter what, we are "precious objects"?

LEARNING TO RECOGNIZE YOUR SELF-WORTH

In every aspect of our lives, we are always asking ourselves, How am I of value? What is my worth? Yet I believe that worthiness is our birthright.

Oprah Winfrey

Self-compassion and self-nurturing are connected to your ability to accept who you are. Self-acceptance means:

- Honoring your experiences, and recognizing that you are doing your best, moment by moment.

- Offering yourself unconditional love, exactly as you are.

- Being willing to be gentle and considerate to yourself.

In turn, self-acceptance is dependent on a sense of self-worth. I believe that self-worth is something you are born with, based on the concept that you have value simply because you exist.

You *deserve* to be here because you *are* here.

Having a healthy sense of self-worth means that you are able to appreciate who you are, regardless of your failures and successes. You recognize your weaknesses and limitations, but you do not let that recognition interfere with your desire and ability to care about yourself and wish yourself well.

Having self-worth does not mean that you are arrogant and that you compare yourself to others in a judgmental way. Rather, it is having the understanding that nobody is perfect and that you deserve to be nice to yourself *simply because you are human*. It is realizing that each human is unique, each human has a basic worth, and that each human has an essence that is worthy of love, no matter what.

Unfortunately, we often lose our sense of self-worth as we encounter people who judge us when we don't live up to their expectations. This often begins with our parents or care-givers. Whether implicitly or excplicitly, we learn that there are aspects of ourselves that are unacceptable or unlovable. It might be the look of disappointment on a parent's face when we bring home a B plus intead of an A. Or the scolding we get if we come in second place at a competition. Or, later as a teen-ager, the pushback we receive when we tell our parents that we want to become a massage therapist or go work on an organic farm.

It is not hard to pick up on the expectations of our parents. Since we are young and are greatly influenced by the adults in our lives, we take those messages into our hearts. We then carry those beliefs with us into adulthood.

So now is the time to begin to challenge our self-judgments. It is easy to look back and criticize ourselves for the decisions we have made in our lives. It is easy to be disappointed or frustrated with ourselves. It is easy to believe that we are only lovable when we do certain things and not others.

It is important for you to create your own message for yourself about what it means to be human. Your philosophy should allow you to connect with a sense of unconditional love. The kind of love and acceptance you needed to hear from your parents or caregivers when you were growing up. The message that no matter what you did and how you did it, you were still loveable and perfect just the way you are.

For example, think about how you might feel if you told yourself this:

"I am a human being. I am not perfect. It is not fair for other people to expect that I be perfect. I am doing my best with what I have moment by moment. That is all I can expect of myself. And in doing so, I love and accept myself as I am."

How might your own version read? Please use your journal to create a similar statement that you can use to remind yourself that you are worthy and loveable.

FINDING THE HERO WITHIN

A hero is someone who has given his or her life to something bigger than oneself.

Joseph Campbell

A hero is somebody who voluntarily walks into the unknown.

Tom Hanks

A hero is an ordinary individual who finds the strength to persevere and endure in spite of overwhelming obstacles.

Christopher Reeve

In your journal, please answer the following questions:

1. What is your personal definition of a "hero"?

2. Who are 3 people, past or present, that you admire? For each one, please list three reasons why you admire them.

3. Whom do you personally know that you would consider a hero? Please explain why.

4. Describe a time you did something that someone else might consider "heroic."

The following journal exercises will assist you in re-connecting with your inherent self-worth. They are designed to give you the opportunity to see yourself as a person worthy of self-compassion and love, simply because of who you are at the deepest level. After all, there is more to you than you might give yourself credit for. It's easy to focus on our failures and shortcomings. Our regrets and 'if-onlys."

So instead, I'd like you to remember and describe in detail those times in your life when you acted like the hero you are.

Please free-write on the following topics:

A time when you acted in a generous way

A time when you did something thoughtful for another person

Three nice things you have done for others

How you have been a good friend or care-taker (either to a person or animal)

A time when you were sensitive to another person's needs

A time when you really cared about doing something the right way

A time when you went above and beyond what was called for

A time when you extended yourself to another, even though you didn't need to

Make a list of five things you like about yourself

Make a list of five things you have done in your life that you are proud of

What makes you different from other people?

What are some risks have you taken? How did they turn out?

What are 3 challenges that you have had to overcome?

List 3 fears (big or small) that you have faced and overcome

What is the hardest thing you have ever had to overcome?

What makes you a survivor?

How have you made a difference (big or small) in another person's life?

I'd like you to answer the following journal questions in more detail. Imagine you are telling a story to someone who is really interested in your life and what you've been through...

What was a setback or obstacle in your life that you eventually overcame? How did you do it? What did you learn from your experience? Begin your story at its lowest point. Then describe what happened from there.

Think of a lesson you have learned in your life. Describe what happened that allowed (or forced) you to learn it. How did learning that lesson impact the rest of your life from that point forward?

Have you ever done something that you were initially afraid of doing? If so, please tell a story about it. Why were you afraid? What allowed you to successfully face your fear? What was that experience like? How did you feel afterwards? What did you learn about yourself?

We've all heard the expression, "Every cloud has a silver lining." Has something bad ever happened to you that later turned out to have at least a small positive impact on your life? Please describe the initial negative event, and then give some details about its "silver lining."

What's the toughest thing you've ever done? How did you handle it? What did you learn about yourself? Looking back, would you have done anything differently?

What are you most proud of in your life? Why?

***

SELF-COMPASSION EXERCISE

Here is a strategy for connecting with your own sense of self-compassion, using the power of your imagination. This is an important exercise because many people have not had the experience of receiving compassion and kindness.

Make sure you can be in a space where you won't be disturbed. Read over these instructions first in order to become familiar with them. Have your journal out where you can access it easily. When you are ready, you can either lay or sit down. The most important thing is that you are comfortable. You can close your eyes during this exercise or keep them open, whichever you prefer.

1. Think about a relationship you have had in the past or have in the present, either with a person or an animal, that is meaningful to you. Now imagine that this person or animal is in need and that you can help it by being kind and compassionate. Take some time to access those feelings.

2. Notice where in your body you have those sensations of kindness and compassion for another. Take as much time as you need to pay attention to where those feelings are residing. When you are ready, place your hands on that spot. Allow yourself to really **notice** what those sensations feel like with your hands. Perhaps you notice a temperature change. Or a tingling. It's different for each person.

3. Now choose a spot on or in your body where you think it would be natural for you to receive compassion. Follow your intuition in picking this spot. For example, it could be your heart. Or your belly. Or your whole body.

4. Imagine gently directing that energy - and that feeling - toward that location with your hands. Spend some time with your hands on that spot. Notice how it feels when compassion and kindness are moving in **your** direction. Notice how it feels when **you** are the one who is giving that to yourself.

5. When you are ready, give yourself permission to allow an image or symbol to coalesce in your mind's eye that reflects these feelings of self-compassion and kindness.

6. Notice its details; its color(s); texture; shape; size.

7. Ask this form if it is OK for you to ask it some questions.

8. Ask it:
    - o How can you assist me?
    - o What can you teach me?
    - o How can I fully experience you?
    - o What message do you have for me?

9. When you are ready, return back to your alert, waking state. Write as much as you can remember in your journal. What have you learned about yourself? How will you integrate what you have learned from this experience into your daily life?

GETTING "SELFISH" ABOUT SELF-CARE

I have found that people often feel guilty about being nice to themselves because doing so somehow means that they are "selfish". This is an obstacle to self-compassion that it is time to address.

People generally find it easier to show compassion and kindness to another person or animal than to themselves. So I'd like you now to think of something or someone that you have loved unconditionally—a pet, stuffed animal, friend, parent, partner, or child. I'm sure you can do this, since you just did so in the previous exercise. You know that when you love someone or something unconditionally, it means that there are no strings attached. You will always love and want the best for that person or animal no matter what they do to you or someone else. You might disapprove of their actions or be disappointed by something they did, but you still love and care about them. And you especially won't hesitate to attend to that person or animal when you see that they are in need.

So what gets in the way of showing that same compassion to yourself? An answer I typically hear is: "I feel like I am being selfish if I pay attention to myself." But I believe that paying attention to yourself and giving yourself nurturing is not selfish. This is because you need to balance the energy you give out to others with energy that you take in for yourself. If you continually give away your energy, eventually you will end up depleted. That is why it is not selfish to rejuvenate. If you identify as a helper, or are a parent, remember: in order to be of assistance, you need energy!

Think about it this way: Your energy is like a full cup of water. And every time you pay attention to others or help them out, you are draining a bit of that water. If you aren't doing something on a regular basis to keep that cup full, eventually it will run dry. Empty. And that won't be good either for you or for those around you.

If other people do not respect your need to replenish your energy, they are giving you clear feedback about their lack of concern for your well-being. This is why **boundaries** are so important. Boundaries are standards and limits a person sets in order to let others know what behavior is acceptable or unacceptable. By being clear to others about your needs, you are teaching people how to treat you; what you will or will not tolerate. In that way, your boundaries act as your protection. You will be able to take care of yourself by setting and maintaining boundaries – and by making sure that other people respect them.

Please answer the following questions in your journal:

How are you boundaries currently being tested or violated? How does that make you feel?

Is there a boundary that you need to create or strengthen? How might you go about doing so?

If you are not willing to set and maintain boundaries, then what is it that you are afraid of?

How easy is it for you to be "selfish"?

If you are "selfish," what are you afraid will happen?

Why is OK to sacrifice your own needs for taking care of others?

What is difficult about saying "no" when somebody asks you to do something for them?

Why is it OK to give but not to receive?

What could you tell yourself that would make it easier for you to attend to your own needs?

What could you tell yourself that would make it easier for you to say "no" to somebody (if doing so is in your best interests)? What message could you tell yourself that would release you from feeling guilty afterwards?

How easy is it for you to tell yourself, "I am worth it"? What would make it easier?

Do you feel guilty when you do something nice for yourself? Why? What are you telling yourself?

What could you say to challenge that part of you that makes you feel guilty about doing nice things for yourself?

When somebody gives you a complement, how do you respond? Is it easy for you to accept it? If it is difficult, what gets in the way?

What could you tell yourself that would make it easier for you to accept a compliment?

Now let's get a sense of how you are doing in terms of self-care:

How do you currently show yourself affection? How have you done so in the past?

How do you currently show yourself appreciation? How have you done so in the past?

What do currently you do for fun? What have you done in the past?

What do you currently do for relaxation? What are some other things that you could do for relaxation that you haven't yet tried?

What currently gives you pleasure? What have you done in the past that has given you pleasure?

***

There are many ways to nurture yourself. Here are some journal prompts to get you started. The answers will provide you with plenty of ideas you can use to bring self-care into your life.

What are some people, places and things that bring a smile to your face?

List 10 things that you have enjoyed doing in the past

List 10 things you currently enjoy doing

List 10 ways to recharge your batteries

My perfect day would be:

Finally, complete this sentence: If I had enough time, I would:

Based on what you've written above, please answer the following questions:

What is something you can do to nourish yourself today?

What is the smallest thing you can do today to make yourself feel good?

What are three things you can commit to doing this week to nurture yourself?

What is something you could do in the next month to "recharge your batteries"?

What or who would you like to add to your life?

What or who would you like to drop from your life?

Make a list of the top ten things you will no longer be doing or accepting in your life as you move forward with your recovery

***

Now I'd like you to create a self-compassion statement or mantra. What can you tell yourself in order to nourish and sustain those feelings of self-care and kindness? Here are some examples:

Accept where you are, accept what you have, accept who you are – do what you can with all of that and let it be enough. (Nikki Rowe)

You've been criticising yourself for years and it hasn't worked. Try approving of yourself and see what happens. (Louise Hay)

Taking good care of yourself means the people in your life receive the best of you rather than what is left of you. (Lucille Zimmerman)

You cannot serve from an empty vessel. (Eleanor Brownn)

...I can understand and be patient with me, just like how I am always understanding and being patient with everyone else. Why? Because I deserve that, and more. (C. Joybell C.)

***

You now should have a bunch of ideas to help you decide how to nurture yourself. Think about how you might incorporate some of those ideas into your life on a daily basis. Create an action plan – and see how easy or difficult it is to follow through. **The key is to start small, since that will create a sense of consistency and success.** Then, as you are able, keep adding!

Here is a challenge for you. Each day for a week, see if you can:

- Notice 5 things that go right
- Pick one way in which to nurture yourself – and do it
- Pick one way to comfort yourself – and do it
- Make a promise to yourself – and keep it
- Do something nice for yourself
- Do something nice for another person or animal

FEELING COMPASSION AND GRATITUDE FOR YOUR BODY

Self-compassion also includes thinking about how your physical body has served you. Take some time to think about what a miracle your body is. It has been working hard for you since before you were even born!

Consider these facts:

- Each day a mature body produces three hundred billion cells in order to replenish and maintain the body's total of seventy-five trillion cells.
- Although your heart weighs less than a pound, it pumps three thousand gallons of blood through you each and every day.
- You are born with about 300 bones but by the time you're an adult you're left with about 200, due to bones fusing together. Your skeleton gives structure to your body, and protects your vital organs.
- Your hand has incredible capabilities, extending and flexing millions of times over a lifetime.
- The marrow of your bones manufacture 2.5 million red blood cells each second, as it works to renew a supply of twenty-five trillion red blood cells.
- Your body has 650 muscles. When you take a step you use two hundred of them (not only in your foot and leg, but also using those in your back and abdomen for balance).
- Every moment of every day your lungs are working. They take in fresh air and expel waste gases in order to bring in the oxygen that is necessary for every cell in your body. At rest you breathe about 12-15 times a minute. That's at least 17,000 breaths in just a single day!
- Your body is continually producing new cells to replace dying cells and to repair damaged ones. When something happens that negatively impacts the integrity of your body (from a sunburn to a small cut to a broken bone), all kinds of healing processes spring into action.
- Then there is your liver. It has over 500 vital processes. In addition, it processes all nutrients absorbed by the intestines and neutralizes toxins. Amazingly, it will still function if up to 80 percent of it is destroyed or cut away, and can rebuild itself in just a few months to its original size!

As you can see, the human body is truly amazing. Unfortunately, it is easy to take our bodies for granted. This is especially true when we are in the depths of our addiction or compulsive behavior. It often is not until we become ill or lose the functioning of a particular body part that we begin to appreciate our physical selves.

Your body exists to serve you, as best it can.

Journal prompts:

How has your body taken care of you in the past?

How does your body currently take care of you?

What can you do to say "Thank you" to your body?

What are some different ways you could acknowledge what your body does for you every day?

How can you recognize and honor what your body has done for you in the past?

How can you use food and eating to honor your body?

YOUR DIGESTIVE SYSTEM

Now I would like to focus on one specific aspect of your internal world: the digestive system. Most of us are divorced from this process – since we can't see inside ourselves, it is easy to ignore what goes on there. But perhaps if we had an idea of what happens to food once we eat it, and how hard our bodies work every minute of every day to digest and use what we eat, we might be able to show our physical selves more kindness.

Our digestive system is a beautifully interconnected network that runs itself. From the time we are born until the day we die, we are continually creating and recreating our bodies through the food we eat. Every moment throughout our lives, our digestive system is working to turn the food we eat into particles that our cells can use for energy, growth, maintenance, and repair.

After taking food into your mouth, chewing begins the digestive process by breaking it down. It is there that one of your most important body fluids comes into play – saliva, produced by the salivary glands. Mostly water, your saliva contains digestive enzymes that initiate the digestion of starches. The liquid nature of saliva allows the bolus (the soft mass of chewed food) to go down the esophagus more easily. In addition, saliva provides an important bath for your mouth! It not only contains minerals that support healthy teeth, but also ensures that your mouth has a proper PH (acid/alkaline) balance.

Next, the food moves down a narrow tube called the esophagus into your stomach. Located under the heart, the stomach turns food into chyme, which is a soupy liquid. Hydorchloric acid, which is produced by cells in the stomach lining, begins to dismantle the proteins in food. It also kills unfriendly microbes in what you've eaten. This acid is strong, but your stomach is protected by a thick coating of mucus. Although most foods pass through the stomach without being fully assimilated into your body, alcohol, water, and some salts enter the bloodstream directly from the stomach.

From the stomach food enters your small intestine, which if stretched out to its full length would measure on average 15 to 20 feet. This is where food is digested and absorbed into the blood stream. The intestinal lining also blocks the absorption of particles that are considered "foreign substances," which are then earmarked for elimination by the body.

Your pancreas has two main roles. First, it helps to neutralize the acidity of the chyme so that it does not burn the tissues of the intestines. Second, it creates and secretes enzymes that digest fats, carbohydrates and protein, which then allow them to be absorbed into the bloodstream.

The liver plays a crucial role in digestion and typically works overtime. It creates bile which emulsifies fats for digestion; makes and breaks down many hormones, including cholesterol, estrogen, and testosterone; regulates blood sugar levels; and processes all of the food – and other materials – which enter your blood stream. The liver acts on nutrients in order to make them usable to your body's cells.

The gall bladder, which lies just below the liver, stores and concentrates the bile which is produced by the liver. Bile breaks down fats, cholesterol, and fat-soluble vitamins into particles that are then easier for digestion.

After all the nutrients have been absorbed, water, fiber and bacteria pass into the large intestine (or colon). This is short, only 3 – 5 feet long. It absorbs water and also forms stool. Trillions of bacteria live in the colon. Its friendly bacteria help your body fight illness and keep you emotionally balanced.

After the stool is well-formed, it gets pushed down into the descending colon and then into the rectum. It remains there until there is enough of it for a bowel movement.

So there you go – the food you eat takes quite a journey through your body, doesn't it! A *lot* is going on every minute of every day inside of you. I believe that if you consider what actually happens to food once you eat it, your relationship with it might change. And perhaps if you understand all of the hard work your body is doing every moment of every day, you would be more inclined to treat it with compassion. Your body is truly doing its best to serve you!

Journal questions:

If your digestive system could communicate, what message would it give you?

How might your knowledge of your digestive system affect what and how you eat?

HONORING YOUR NEEDS

What are needs and how are they connected to self-compassion? I believe that an important way to show yourself kindness is by acknowledging that your needs are valid and deserve to be met.

Tellingly, the word "need" comes from the West Saxon (Old English) noun *nied*, meaning "necessity, compulsion, duty." It is also related to the Czech *nyti* which means "to languish." A need, whether physical or emotional, is something that is necessary for a person's well-being. When a need is fulfilled, we feel healthy and satisfied. Unfulfilled needs leave us with ill-health, frustration and resentment.

As humans, we all share the physical needs of oxygen, water, and food. Different emotional needs, however, will resonate either more strongly or weakly with us because each person is unique. But in varying degrees, most of us have a need to feel:

- Safe and Secure

- Connected with others

- Acknowledged

- A sense of control

- Loved and accepted

- That there is meaning in our life

Our current behaviors, thoughts, and feelings are often generated in response to needs that did not get addressed when we were children. Because they were not filled, these needs continue to haunt us throughout life and into adulthood.

Journal exercises

What did you need as a child from your parents/caregivers that you did not receive?

Imagine that you received the perfect nurturing from your parents. What would they have given you? What would you have heard your parents say to you?

Can you accept having needs without feeling selfish? If not, what are you telling yourself that prevents you? From whom did you learn those messages?

What do you really want?

What are 10 important things for you to do?

What do you need to have?

What do you need to know?

What do you need to do?

What do you hunger for?

What makes you feel loved?

What makes life feel magical?

What is unlived or missing in your life that is required for it to be more complete and whole?

In your journal, make a list of your current needs (Some examples might be: Solitude; having close friendships; adventure; quality time with your children; a fulfilling job; being really listened to by your partner; the opportunity to be creative)

How many of your needs are currently being met?

For each need that is not being met or is not being sufficiently met, please answer:

1. What emotion(s) do you feel when you think about this need not being met?

2. What thoughts come to mind?

3. What behavior(s) do you engage in because that need isn't being met?

4. What is the cost to you of this need not being met?

5. What change(s) would occur in your life if the need were met?

6. What has to happen for the need to be met?

7. How can you strengthen your commitment to fulfilling that need?

***

Now let's address the needs of your physical body. Please consider each of these statements:

1. My body deserves to be nourished
2. My body deserves to be treated with respect
3. My body deserves to wear comfortable clothing and shoes
4. My body deserves affectionate touch
5. My body deserves to move through the world with ease

What thoughts and feelings come up for you as you read each of these statements? What, if anything, prevents your body from having these needs met? What can you do (on a daily / weekly / monthly basis) to begin to honor the various needs of your body?

FORGIVING YOURSELF

I did then what I knew how to do. Now that I know better, I do better.

Maya Angelou

Another key component to developing self-compassion is the ability to forgive oneself. It is my experience that people often treat themselves poorly because they believe they have to punish themselves for something they did wrong in the past.

Forgiveness means recognizing that there are things that occurred in the past that we cannot change. So first we must release the desire that things had happened differently than they did. This does not necessarily mean accepting what has happened. Rather, it means making peace with the fact that something has happened, and releasing anger, shame and guilt. Until we reach a point where we are ready to forgive, our bitterness and disappointment reside in us as toxic substances, and act as barriers to self-compassion. As Nelson Mandela pointed out, "Resentment is like drinking poison and then hoping it will kill your enemies." Indeed, some people use compulsive behavior (such as cutting) as a means to punish themselves. Because they believe that they deserve to be punished, it is easier for them to treat their bodies poorly.

Take same time to look back over your life and in your journal:

Make a list of things that you regret doing

Make a list of things that you regret not doing

Make a list of things you did that you are angry at yourself about

Make a list of things about which you are ashamed at yourself

For each entry on your lists, ask yourself:

- At that time, what need was I trying to meet?
- What was I thinking to myself?

- What feeling or emotion was I experiencing?

The next step is to accept what happened and to forgive yourself. You can do this by telling yourself:

I was doing the best I could have been doing in that moment. If I could have done something differently, I would have. Therefore, I accept myself without judgment. I was trying to get my needs met in the only way I knew how at that time. I wish it would not have happened but it did. And so I forgive myself. I am willing to move on. I am ready to move forward in my life.

Finally, and perhaps most importantly, for each item on your lists, please fill in the following:

"I am proud of myself because…"

It is also so important to be able to forgive yourself in the present. You have to continually remind yourself that you are doing the best you can in this moment. Always keep in mind the Maya Angelou quote from above: If you could be doing something differently, you would – so give yourself a break!

CULTIVATING GRATITUDE

Let us rise up and be thankful, for if we didn't learn a lot today, at least we learned a little, and if we didn't learn a little, at least we didn't get sick, and if we got sick, at least we didn't die. So let us all be thankful.

the Buddha

Gratitude is connected to a sense of appreciation, recognition, and love for people, places, and things in your life. Gratitude is also a very important factor in creating self-kindness. This is because in order to have self-compassion, you have to be able to *appreciate* who you are and why you are the way you are. By focusing on what you are thankful for, you will shift your attention in a positive direction. As you begin to pay attention to what you appreciate about your life and who you are as a person, it will become easier for you to show yourself compassion. And it will become more difficult to treat yourself poorly.

In your journal, please answer the following:

What is currently going right for you in your life? What's working?

How can you honor what is going right in your life?

What are 20 things or people you are grateful for?

What are the blessings in your life?

Currently in your life:

    What are you happy about?

    What are you excited about?

    What are you proud of?

    What are you *most* grateful for?

    What are you enjoying?

    What are you committed to?

    Whom do you love?

    Who loves you?

A powerful way to connect with gratitude is the next exercise, which was developed by Tony Robbins. Each evening before bed, meditate on or journal about the following three questions. They will provide you with a powerful new perspective that will activate your sense of gratitude.

1. What have I given today?
2. What did I receive today?
3. What did I learn today?

Another effective tool for developing a sense of appreciation and self-compassion is **The Gratitude Journal**.

Each day, at a specific time, in a special journal dedicated solely to this task, center yourself, and then list three things you are thankful for. Of course, if you are feeling inspired, you can certainly list more than three. But your benchmark of success with this ritual is three items, since that is within the realm of possibility for everyone, no matter how busy. Please write as much or as little with each entry as you choose. If you do have the time, though, I believe that writing in more detail about each entry can deepen your sense of gratitude more than a simple list will. I also feel that if you can avoid hurrying through this ritual, you will reap greater benefits. Ideally, as you finish writing each item on your list, you will take some time to savor the gift you have been presented with. Notice how it feels to relish each blessing in your life (no matter how big or small). Try to connect with both an emotional and physical sense of how deep your gratitude runs for each item.

I would like to emphasize that you don't have to think too hard about what to be grateful for. You can list major events in your life if you'd like. Perhaps you're grateful for a raise at work. Or that you finished a marathon. But don't be afraid to write about the simple or mundane things that you generally take for granted, such as being able to take a deep breath without pain. Or the smell of fresh flowers. Or your child's smile. At the same time, perhaps you might want to remind yourself that you have a roof over your head. Or running water. Or that you woke up this morning.

As far as what you actually write, simply follow your intuition. There is no right or wrong way to keep a Gratitude Journal. But to give you a sense of how to start, you could simply use these sentence stems:

"Today I am grateful for…"

"Today I am grateful that…"

The beautiful thing about the ritual of the Gratitude Journal is that with each passing day, you will begin to notice the abundance in your life, rather than the lack. Remember, what you focus on will grow…

In addition, if you start to consider how your life would be without those people or things you are thankful for, your sense of gratitude and well-being will only deepen. And in turn, so will your feelings of compassion, kindness and understanding for yourself.

***

No discussion about gratitude would be complete without including the suggestion of offering thanks before a meal. Most of us are familiar with "saying grace," which comes from the Latin expression "*gratiarum actio*," meaning "an act of thanks." We often think about this is in a religious context, since in the United States saying grace before a meal is associated with Christianity. However, offering a blessing before eating is found universally in all cultures. Certainly, for some people, thanking their Higher Power for its life-giving force or the earth for its bounty is an important devotional ritual. Yet in our fast-paced, hurried and harried world, it is very easy to bypass saying grace, and just jump right into eating.

That is why I would like you to consider saying grace for at least one meal each day. Doing so is a simple way to connect with gratitude and appreciation.

You can begin by thanking God or your Higher Power or Mother Earth. But I also believe it can be a profound experience to spend time before each meal thinking about all of the people whose efforts have led to the food that is sitting on your plate: The farmers, the harvesters, the people who packaged the food, those who transported it, the clerks at the store who shelved it, the person who went out and bought it, and then whoever cooked it. Plus, if you are eating part of an animal, it is important to recognize that it gave its life for your nourishment. And so in that way does each integral part of a long chain deserve your thanks.

Introducing the tradition of saying grace into your life is *powerful*. It forces you to slow down, pay attention, and consider your meal. Eating is the most intimate thing you can do, as the food you consume actually becomes part of your body. That is why the act of saying grace transforms what could be a mundane, rushed or thoughtless act into the sacred, deliberate ritual it truly is.

There is no right or wrong way to say grace. It can be done in silence, spoken, sung – and even signed. I know one family whose members, all together as a group, simply repeat "Thank you" out loud seven or eight times before each meal. Then there are the multitudes of blessings from religious and cultural traditions, ranging from the simple "Bless this food," to lengthy prayers.

The bottom line is this: If you choose to begin to say grace before each meal, think about the words that resonate with you. Remember, this isn't about going through the motions. Rather, it is about communicating a heart-felt sense of gratitude for the opportunity (and privilege) to eat a meal. Thus, the best mealtime prayers will flow spontaneously as you follow your intuition and trust your soul to provide the right words for you.

CHAPTER 6

Being of Service

The best way to find yourself is to lose yourself in the service of others.

Gandhi

As you know, a universal truth is that what you choose to focus on, grows. There is no better way to connect with a sense of purpose and meaning than by turning your attention to others. As you move along your journey of recovery, volunteering is a way for you to feel proud, because you are doing something over which you actually do have control: Making a real difference in the life of another person or animal. What a way to strengthen your feeling of self-worth! Volunteering is especially useful because all of that energy that you used to use engaging in and managing your addiction can now be used in a more productive, life-affirming way.

In addition, by shifting your focus away from yourself and onto others, you'll avoid isolation, develop positive relationships and help to improve your community. Being a volunteer will allow you to put things in perspective and see how we are all connected.

Check out these statistics from a study the United Health Group conducted in 2013. Based on the answers of 3351 adults, of those who had volunteered in the prior 12 months:

- 76% reported that doing so made them feel healthier.

- 94% said that being a volunteer improved their mood.

- 78% stated that volunteering lowered their level of stress.

- 96% said that helping others "enriches their sense of purpose in life."

Please answer the following questions in your journal:

Have you volunteered in the past? If so, what did you do? What was that experience like?

Are you currently volunteering? If so, how is that experience going for you? If not, what prevents you from doing so?

What social causes are you most passionate about?

What makes you angry?

What is one thing you could do this week to help another person or animal?

What is one thing you could in the next month to help another person or animal?

If money and time weren't an issue, what would be your ideal volunteer experience? Why? What are three things you could do now, which are within your power, that would bring you closer to making that a reality?

Inventory #2

Let's take a quick inventory of your life again, just like you did at the beginning of the program. How have things been going?

Sleep

1--10

Family Relationships

1--10

Intimate Relationship(s)

1--10

Relationship with Children

1--10

Physical Health

1---10

Mental Health

1---10

Relationship with God / Higher Power

1---10

Spirituality / Religion

1---10

Work/Career

1---10

Finances

1---10

Leisure Time / Relaxation

1---10

Hobbies / Things you do for fun

1---10

Food

1---10

Education / School

1---10

Relationships with Friends

1---10

Legal Issues

1---10

Energy Level

1---10

Optimism about the Future

1---10

For each area of your life, in order to increase your score by just a single point, what can you:

Do more of?

Do less of?

Start?

Stop?

CHAPTER 7

Overcoming Maladaptive Beliefs

Most of us have become so accustomed to acting out our internal version of ourselves that we are no longer aware that just because we believe something doesn't make it true. Just because we've been living according to particular beliefs for twenty or fifty years does not mean they have one shred of validity...

Geneen Roth

We don't see things as they are, we see them as we are.

Anais Nin

I asked myself, 'What is the myth you are living?' and found that I did not know. So...I took it upon myself to get to know 'my' myth and regarded this as the task of tasks...I simply had to know what unconscious or preconscious myth was forming me.

Carl Jung

A belief system is the particular set of stories and understandings that we have about ourselves and the world around us. In short, it is the framework within which we define and experience *reality*. Carol Pearson notes,

Our experience quite literally is defined by our assumptions about life...We make stories about the world and to a large degree live out their plots. What our lives are like depends to a great extent on the script we consciously, or more likely, unconsciously, have adopted.

It is vital that you seek to understand the belief system that governs your life. You can do so by examining the values, assumptions, ideals and ideologies which influence (and limit) the way you think, feel and act. Once you have gained insight into how you process reality, you can then decide if it is necessary to reprogram yourself with a new belief system that serves your best interests. The key to unlocking a negative belief system is understanding that *you were not born with it*. You learned it as a child. Therefore, it is not your fate. It can be changed. *You* can change it.

One discovers that destiny can be directed, that one does not have to remain in bondage to the first imprint made on childhood sensibilities. Once the deforming mirror has been smashed, there is a possibility of wholeness. There is a possibility of joy.

Anais Nin

Therefore, a very important question to ask yourself is:

Where did my basic assumptions and ideas about myself and the world around me originate?

Often you learned these assumptions and ideas from the same people and places that provided you with your original value system:

- Societal norms
- Family
- The media
- Community (peers; friends; religious institutions; teachers)
- Feedback from our own experiences

So consider this: What you believe to be "reality" might simply be a collection of ideas, perceptions, assumptions, expectations, and opinions that you have come to accept about you and the world around you. In other words, just because you believe it, doesn't mean – or make it – real.

Remember, our basic assumptions frame the world we live in and provide the meaning we find in it. But most of us are not conscious of those assumptions. And what's worse, these assumptions may actually be *misperceptions* because they are arbitrary, taught to us by people who weren't capable of doing anything other than projecting their own baggage onto their children. So let's take as an example the belief that "The world is a dangerous place." Is that reality? Or is it something a parent learned based on their own experiences, which they then passed down to their child as *The Truth*.

And so the problem of beliefs is that they can prevent us from seeing things as they really are. It's like they form a veil over objective reality. That is, instead of spontaneously *responding* to something in an appropriate manner, we automatically *react* the way we have *always* reacted. "You're inviting me to go with you to Mexico City?" [automatic internal reaction: "Of course I won't go – too dangerous! Anywhere I'm not familiar with – too dangerous. The world – too dangerous...] More appropriate response: "Sounds great but let me think about it." [and after doing some research then discovering that depending where you go in Mexico City it actually is quite safe]

In that sense, beliefs keep us trapped in the past like a fly in amber. And that is the tragedy: our belief systems are like specially tinted glasses crafted decades ago that prevent us from truly *seeing* reality. The result is that we fail to engage with what is in front of us on a moment-by-moment basis. Instead we use programming from faulty programmers to pre-judge. Because our minds are already made up.

Please read through the following examples of beliefs. Notice if any sound familiar to you.

- Winners never quit.
- People can't be trusted.
- Women shouldn't work.
- Men aren't dependable.
- Life isn't fair.
- I am a bad person.
- I will never fit in.
- I am incapable of being independent.
- I am weak.
- I need other people to validate me.
- I should be able to do whatever I want.
- It's always my fault.
- It's never my fault.
- My needs don't matter.
- It is OK for me to deprive myself.
- It's best to take care of others.
- My worth is based on other people's opinions of me.
- Life is hard.
- It's not good to show emotions.
- I always should be perfect.
- It's not good to make mistakes.
- Success means being materially wealthy.
- When good things happen, something bad is never far behind.
- Asking others for help is a sign of weakness.
- Boys don't cry.
- Wives should defer to their husbands.
- Divorce should never be an option.
- Money is the root of all evil.
- A person's worth is based on how hard they work.
- You can never depend on other people to come through.
- Help from others always comes with strings attached.
- Showing your intelligence is a sign of arrogance.

In your journal, please answer the following:

1. What do you believe to be true about yourself?

2. What do you believe to be true about other people?

3. What do you believe to be true about the world?

4. Where did you learn each of those beliefs?

Now, using a separate page in your journal, I would like you to answer the following questions for each one:

1. What has this belief helped me to accomplish?
2. What has this belief helped me to avoid?
3. What does this belief allow me to do?
4. What does this belief allow me to have?
5. What does this belief allow me to be?
6. What are the advantages of this belief?
7. How do I use this belief against others?
8. What has this belief gotten me into?
9. What has this belief gotten me out of?
10. What has this belief solved?
11. When would this belief be a good idea?
12. When would this belief not be a good idea?

Finally: Each of your rules and beliefs has consequences. For each one, please answer the following two questions.

1. What happens when I have this belief?
2. What would happen if I didn't have this belief?

Now go back and take an inventory of your beliefs. Get a sense of which ones expand the possibilities in your life and give you energy. Notice the ones which limit you and drain your energy.

To avoid self-sabotage as you make changes in your life, it is necessary for you to understand the role your beliefs have played in determining your perspective on life. You must remind yourself that you do not have to be a slave to your beliefs – they are not set in stone.

So having lived your life with a particular belief system – and knowing how it has affected you – what would you change about it? Which beliefs would you like to keep? Which would you like to release? And what might be some new empowering beliefs about the world that you could add?

This is your chance to create a supportive belief framework as you move forward with your recovery. Here are some examples of beliefs that will make your journey easier:

- I deserve to be loved.
- I am a worthwhile human being.
- I am unique.
- I have faith in myself.
- I can trust my body.
- It is OK to make mistakes.
- It is OK to be nice to myself.
- I am open to new experiences.
- I am stronger than I realize.
- I won't let perfect get in the way of good enough.
- It is OK to take risks.
- I don't have to be perfect.
- I am strong enough to love another person.
- It is OK for me to receive love and support.
- It is important for me to show my emotions.
- I am willing to make mistakes as long as I learn from them.
- I don't need approval from other people.
- I am comfortable trusting my intuition.
- People can change.
- The world is a supportive, giving place.
- Success is being content with what I already have.

Journal Exercise

Make a list of the beliefs that you would like to consciously bring into your life. These are beliefs that support you, empower you, and allow you to be kind to yourself. After all, if you are going to have a belief system anyway (as human beings we can't escape it), you might as well have one that doesn't lead to feelings of guilt, shame, or unworthiness. If you would like, you can also write a manifesto, create a collage or make some other artwork that expresses your new world view.

It might take time for your new belief system to truly sink in because you have been living with your old one for so many years. Please be patient and take the time to remind yourself *why* you have decided to modify your core beliefs. An easy way to do that is by reviewing the exercises you did in this chapter. As you begin to feel better and see how your relationship with your addiction or compulsive behavior is shifting, your new perspective will reinforce itself.

CHAPTER 8

Neutralizing Negative Self-Talk

The mind is everything. What you think, you become.

the Buddha

To enjoy good health, to bring true happiness to one's family, to bring peace to all, one must first discipline and control one's own mind.

the Buddha

Another road-block that gets in the way of positive change is **negative thinking**. Everyone has voices in their heads – that's just part of being human. It is natural to carry on a conversation with ourselves in our minds, and most of us do this all the time.

However, our mental chatter sometimes communicates things that make us feel badly about ourselves or our lives. These negative thoughts lead to feelings such as depression, anxiety, and low self-esteem. We often take our distressing inner monologue seriously because it sounds rational and accurate.

Our negative thinking prevents us from leaving behind the addictions and compulsions in our lives because it scares us and reaffirms the negative views we have of the world. As you will learn, however, those negative thoughts are flawed, and by believing them you buy into the maladaptive core beliefs we discussed in the last chapter.

The skill you will learn in this chapter is how to recognize and address those negative thoughts (also known as "cognitive distortions"), so that they do not control your life or limit your choices. The good news is that because your negative thinking is learned, you can un-learn it.

At this point, you might be wondering about the differences between your core negative belief system and your negative thinking. Think of your belief system as the foundation of your house. It is the base that supports and gives shape to the entirety of the home itself. Depending on how that foundation was constructed, your house will have a particular structure. Your negative thinking is represented by specific rooms in your house. Just as a home has many kinds of rooms, from small to large, so too do you have many different types of negative thoughts (which I will describe in more detail below).

So your core belief system is a general way of looking at the world, while your negative thinking consists of particular thoughts that are triggered when specific things happen to you.

For example, let's say that one of your core negative beliefs is "I am a failure," because a parent continually told you that "You can't do anything right." Your negative self-talk will support that belief. When you do poorly on a test you tell yourself, "See, I knew that was going to happen, I'm just not a good student." Or you'll decide not to try out for the softball team, telling yourself, "There's no way I could be good at that." Or when your supervisor at work gives you negative feedback (even if done in a constructive way) you become depressed and think to yourself, "This job is too much for me – I should never have taken it. I'm in over my head. I'll never get the hang of it. I am sure they are going to fire me."

HOW TO DISCOVER YOUR "IRRATIONAL THOUGHTS"

In psychology, we often refer to negative thoughts as "irrational" because they have no basis in objective reality. For example, you may tell yourself, "I don't want to go to that party because I know I'll have a bad time." This thought certainly appears real to you and generates feelings of shame and sadness. But consider this – there is no way to predict the future, which is exactly what you are doing. All negative thinking can be debunked once you challenge its logic. That is why we would call that thought about not wanting to go to the party "irrational."

In order to address your negative beliefs, you must first figure out what your inner monologue actually consists of. The easiest way to do this is by paying attention to the negative messages that you tell yourself as you go through the day. This is when your mindfulness skills will really pay off. Once you are able to recognize those thoughts for what they really are, then you can begin to challenge them. And by neutralizing your negative thinking, you will discover that you have the ability to avoid many of the negative emotions you are used to having. You will also experience a sense of openness and possibility, since you will be able to avoid the constraints your negative thinking imposes on you. And your path to recovery will become all the easier.

In the next section I provide a list of the most common cognitive distortions. I would like you to become familiar with this list. Doing so will help you become aware of the patterns of your own negative thinking. You'll also see that you are not crazy – everyone has negative thoughts that fall into one or more of these categories. You are not alone!

EXAMPLES OF COGNITIVE DISTORTIONS

Psychologists have discovered that negative thoughts can be grouped into categories based on particular characteristics. As you notice what you tell yourself each day, you can use the list below to "label" your thinking. You will discover that your thoughts will most likely fall into at least one of the following categories. Once you recognize that your thought is "irrational" and not a true reflection of reality, you will see it for what it is, and thereby weaken its power over you.

Each category has a specific example of irrational thinking in action. I have also included a "more helpful response" that will help you to see alternative ways of dealing with an event. I worded these "responses" in such a way as to give you an idea of what you might tell or ask yourself in those situations.

ALL OR NOTHING THINKING

You use rigid categories that lead to either/or conclusions; there is no in-between. You think in absolutes such as "always," and "never," which means that you don't believe in exceptions.

> **Example:** You go on a diet and then sneak a "forbidden food." This makes you feel awful because you believe you've just ruined the entire diet; you've failed.

> **More helpful response:** "Things aren't either totally white or totally black – there are shades of grey. Where is this on the spectrum? Is it *really* true that I've **failed** at this diet? How can I learn from my mistake and move on?"

OVER-GENERALIZING

You draw the conclusion that a single negative event is actually a never-ending pattern. Even though the case might be isolated, you still believe that it applies to every instance.

> **Example:** You decide to try a new habit but then give up after several weeks. This leads you to berate yourself: "I can *never* stick with anything!"

> **More helpful response:** "Is it true that things are **always** or **never** a certain way? Where are the exceptions? Am I exaggerating?"

MENTAL FILTERING

You focus on a single negative detail about a situation or person, and ignore neutral or positive things.

> **Example:** You go out for an anniversary meal with your partner. The meal itself is delicious – until desert, which is underwhelming. On the way home, all you do is complain about how disappointing the dinner was.

> **More helpful response:** "Am I only noticing the bad stuff? Am I filtering out the positives? What is a more realistic assessment?"

DISQUALIFYING THE POSITIVE

You reject positive experiences, believing that "they don't count". You maintain a negative view in spite of contradictory evidence.

>**Example:** You spend a lot of time cooking and people are always asking you for recipes. But you tell yourself that your food is nothing special, and are skeptical of those who praise it.

>**More helpful response:** "Is there positive feedback I might be ignoring? Why might I not believe something positive that somebody says about me?"

MIND READING

You believe that you know what another person is thinking. Typically this involves arbitrarily deciding that someone is reacting negatively to you.

>**Example:** You are talking to a group of people about your experiences, and notice that one of the people is continually looking at her watch. You assume that she is bored and can't wait for you to stop talking.

>**More helpful response:** "Am I assuming I know what others are thinking? Am I jumping to conclusions? What's the evidence? Those are my own thoughts, not theirs. Is there another, more balanced way of looking at it?"

FORTUNE TELLING

You believe that things will turn out badly in the future, and are convinced that your predictions are actual facts.

>**Example:** You decline an invitation to a party, because you think that you will have a terrible time.

>**More helpful response:** "Do I really believe that I can predict the future? How likely is my prediction to happen? Why do I think I'm going to have a bad time? Where's the evidence for that?"

CATASTROPHIZING

You believe the worst possible outcome will occur. Or you think that things can't be any worse.

Example #1: You decide against going out dancing with your partner because you believe that you'll look stupid, feel humiliated and have a terrible time.

More helpful response: "What's actually most likely to happen? In a past similar situation, did my worst fears occur? For a current situation: Is this as bad as it could be? That is, could it be worse?"

Example #2: Your boss at work give you back a report you'd filed that has some some things you need to correct. You feel humiliated and believe that you're going to be fired.

More helpful response: "Is this really the end of the world? Where is the evidence that making mistakes on this report is going to make me lose my job? How can I learn from this and do better in the future?"

MAGNIFYING OR MINIMIZING

You exaggerate the significance of certain things (such as your mistakes or other people's successes) and minimize other things (such as your own positive qualities or other's imperfections).

Example #1: You enter and win a competition. When people compliment you, you brush them off by replying that your performance was nothing special.

More helpful response: "Thank you!"

Example #2: You're in a band and after your show people compliment you. However, you respond with, "Yeah, but I really messed up that first song, I can't believe I forgot those chords! I'm really disappointed in myself..."

More helpful response: "Thank you!" (odds are that nobody but you remembers what happened during the first song...)

EMOTIONAL REASONING

You assume that the way you feel reflects the way things are. You feel guilty, and therefore believe that you have truly done something bad. Or you feel overwhelmed, and conclude that your problem is truly impossible to solve.

> **Example:** You avoid trying out a new recipe because it looks complicated. The complexity makes you feel anxious, which in turn leads you to believe that the dish is impossible for you to successfully make.

> **More helpful response:** "Just because it *feels* bad, doesn't necessarily mean it *is* bad. My feelings are just a reaction to my thoughts. Where is the evidence that once I start in on the recipe, it won't go better than I originally thought?"

SHOULDS

You believe things must or must not be a certain way. "Shoulds" act as inflexible rules and standards about the way the world is supposed to work.

> **Example #1:** As a woman, I should look a certain way, or others won't find me attractive. ("Shoulds" aimed at yourself can lead to feelings of guilt.)

> **Example #2:** A real man shouldn't cry. I can't believe I let people see that I was tearing up during that movie! ("Shoulds" directed toward others may lead to disappointment, anger, or resentment.)

> **More helpful response:** "What kind of pressure am I putting on myself? Am I setting up expectations for myself or others that are impossible to meet? Where did I learn my "shoulds" from? What would be more realistic standards for myself? For others?"

LABELING / MISLABELING

Sometimes, when you have made a mistake, you get angry at yourself and call yourself a bad name. That is, instead of focusing on what you actually did, you give yourself a label that reflects your entire being. Some common labels are "idiot," "stupid," "good-for-nothing," and "ugly."

> **Example:** Your work presentation didn't go as well as you had hoped. So you call yourself "a loser."

> **More helpful response:** "Am I labeling myself? Is it fair to sum up my entire existence with just one single word? Can I explore how I am much more than a label? Why do I need to beat myself up for making a mistake?"

PERSONALIZATION

You see yourself as responsible for events around you that you have no control over. This often leads to deep guilt. The other side of this distortion is externalization: this is when you believe that other people have complete control of your life, whereas you have none. This results in blaming others for your situation, while not recognizing the role you are playing.

> **Example #1:** Your child is bullied at school. You immediately blame yourself for what happened.

> **More helpful response:** "Am I jumping to conclusions about my role in an incident? How do I know that I was responsible for what happened? Where is the evidence?"

> **Example #@:** Every time you watch a certain reality TV show featuring wealthy people, you feel inadequate about your life and become depressed.

> **More helpful response:** "How much power am I giving this TV show over my feelings? How am recognizing my choice whether or not to watch this program?"

PAYING ATTENTION TO YOUR OWN THINKING

For the next week, pay attention to what you tell yourself each day. See which things really set off your inner monologue. Notice the connection between something happening and subsequent negative emotions such as guilt, shame, sadness or frustration. At that moment, do an internal check-in and listen closely to what you are saying to yourself. Based on the list of cognitive distortions above, see which categories your negative thinking falls into.

In your journal, I would like you to write down some examples of your negative thinking, along with their categories (for example, mind-reading or catastrophizing).

For each negative thought, please consider the following two questions:

Does this support me or help me achieve my goals in life?

Or does this line of thinking create pain?

***

As you begin to notice your patterns of negative self-talk, please consider the following questions:

- o Where might you have learned the self-talk that goes on in your head?

- o When you have a thought about yourself or your life, how do you know that what you are thinking is absolutely true?

- o If your self-talk was influenced by another person, could there have been something going on in that person's life that affected how she or he talked to you?

MORE WAYS TO CHALLENGE YOUR IRRATIONAL THOUGHTS

When something happens that triggers your negative thoughts (which then creates distressing emotions), it is up to you to immediately do two things:

1. Recognize what is happening

2. Refuse to be held hostage by your thinking

The key is to take a time out. Stop, pause, and take a deep breath. Notice how your thinking is affecting your emotions. If you see that you are engaging in negative thinking, silently tell yourself to "Stop it." You can use a calm voice to do so, or you can shout down those negative voices in an assertive, tough tone. If it is more helpful, visualize a large Stop sign that halts your irrational thoughts in their tracks. The important thing is to quickly cut off or drown out any irrational thoughts that have made an appearance. Then ask yourself, "Am I responding appropriately to the situation? Or am I having a knee-jerk reaction that is based on my past experiences? How rational is my thinking here? What is the evidence that these thoughts are actually true?"

Show yourself some compassion and remind yourself that you don't have to react automatically to a situation. It is perfectly fine to step back and deliberate how to respond. As you will see, there are some powerful questions you can ask yourself that will take the wind out of the sails of your negative thoughts.

The list below provides you with questions that can help you refute your irrational thinking. You don't have to memorize all of them. Rather, go through the list and choose four or five that resonate with you. Those will be your go-to questions to ask yourself in order to determine whether or not your thinking is accurate and fair.

- What am I reacting to?
- What do I think is going to happen here?
- What's the worst (and best) that could happen? What's most likely to happen?
- How helpful is it for me to think this way?
- Am I getting things out of proportion?
- Are these negative feelings worth it?
- How important is this really? How important will it be next week? Next month? In 6 months?
- What meaning am I giving this situation?
- Am I overestimating things?
- Am I underestimating my ability to deal with this situation?
- Is there another way I could look at this?
- What could be influencing my interpretation of the situation?
- What advice would I give to a friend in this same situation?
- How much of this situation is within my control? What is outside my control?
- How can I address – even in a small way – things that are under my control?
- What will be the consequences of reacting the way I typically do?
- Could there be another way of dealing with this?
- What would be the most helpful thing to do right now?
- Right now, what is the most effective action I can take?
- What is the evidence that supports my thinking? What is the evidence against it?
- How logically am I thinking this through?
- Am I thinking in a black and white manner?

- Is my source of information trustworthy?
- Would somebody else come to the same conclusions I have?
- Is my thought really 100% true?
- How do I know this thought is really true?

THE "SHOULD" TRAP

Especially watch out when the word "should" runs through your head. A "should" or "should not" typically refers to an inflexible rule or a rigid way of viewing reality. This kind of thinking limits you and causes suffering because it is not responsive to the present moment. Instead, it is based on some standard that was created in another time and place by someone else. This leads to you feeling pressure, and then guilt, if you can't measure up to the "should."

For example:

- I should look a certain way
- I shouldn't have made that mistake
- I should have known that answer
- I should always keep my home clean and tidy
- I should get married and have children
- I should always be on time
- I should always get my way
- I should spend more time at work
- I should buy that item because it's on sale
- I should exercise three times a week
- I shouldn't eat between meals
- I should eat that kind of food because it is healthy for me
- I shouldn't have eaten that donut because I should have known better
- I should have have a "respectable" career
- I should always be helpful
- I shouldn't say "no"
- I shouldn't fail
- I shouldn't be vulnerable
- I should always come out on top

Of course, some "shoulds" are good for you. Ones like "I should brush my teeth," "I shouldn't stay up all night" and "I should save at least *some* of my money ever month" will lead you in the direction of health and prevent suffering. That is why it is important to spend time considering which of your "should" statements reflect beliefs that do – or do not – serve your best interests.

So, what are *your* "shoulds"? Please take some time to think about this. Consider some of the rules you have in your life about how you (and other people) should or shouldn't behave or be. As you come up with them, list each one out in your journal.

From whom or what did you learn each of your "shoulds"?

How does each of your "shoulds" benefit your life?

How does each of your "shoulds" limit your life?

Do any of your "shoulds" cause you suffering?

Are there any "shoulds" that it is time to retire?

Are there any "shoulds" to add to your list that might empower you?

POSITIVE SELF-TALK

By disputing your irrational thoughts, you will be able to see situations more objectively. This prevents you from being sucked into negative emotions. But that isn't the end of the story. It is important to replace your negative thinking with thoughts that are positive and affirming. This is because you will encounter challenges and stresses as you go through life. Stress is part of living that we all have to deal with, so you shouldn't seek to avoid it. Rather, your goal is to be able to handle stressful or new or negative situations in a healthy productive way. Your positive self-talk will get you through difficult times and help you to avoid the suffering caused by irrational thinking. By improving your outlook and developing resilience, you'll be able to better handle stress and uncertainty in your life.

An easy way to come up with positive self-talk is to ask yourself what a good friend would say to you about the situation you're dealing with. Think about words that would support and encourage you, make you feel safe and validated, and that would motivate you.

Here are some examples of switching out negative thinking with positive self-talk:

- **Instead of** "I'm scared because I've never done this before," ***reframe it*** as "This is a chance for me to learn something new."

- Instead of "This is too hard for me, I'm giving up," reframe it as "This is unfamiliar to me right now. I will see which of my friends I can ask for help."

- Instead of "I don't have enough money to travel. Just forget it," reframe it as "I will brainstorm ideas to make my trip happen. Maybe there are some ways to find the resources that I haven't thought of yet."

- Instead of "This change in my life is pretty scary; I feel powerless," reframe it as "I will do my best to prepare myself for this change."

- Instead of "I'm afraid that I won't be able to handle the stress of living in a new city," reframe it as "I will cross those bridges when I come to them."

- Instead of "I feel like I don't have any friends," reframe it as "What can I do from my end to begin to meet new people? Are there any groups or clubs I'm interested in that I can join?"

- Instead of "Learning this skill is frustrating, I"ll never get it," reframe it as "Why don't I take a break and come back to this later? That way I'll feel fresh."

- Instead of "I just can't do this," reframe it as "What can I do or learn to ensure that I *will* be able to do this? Other people have managed to learn how to do this – so will I!"

- Instead of "Look at everyone else – they are much better than I am," reframe it as "Considering my level of training, I think I'm doing fine. I'll get to their level as long as I continue to practice."

- Instead of "I'm really nervous about my piano recital tonight – I don't want to go," reframe it as "Let me just focus on what is happening in each moment and let go of projecting into the future. All I have control over is what is happening right now. I'm just going to keep breathing to keep myself grounded, and I'll be fine."

I also recommend that you develop an all-purpose saying or mantra that you can use to get you through a tough time. One of my favorites is "This too shall pass." I use it when I feel that there is no end in sight to something that is disturbing me. But because I know that everything changes, I make sure to remind myself that nothing – whether good or bad – lasts forever.

The phrase "What can I learn from this?" also regularly helps me find the silver lining in an otherwise negative situation. Or, "Based on what's going on, what is my next best step?"

Another idea is to hum part of your favorite inspirational song when you are feeling down. For me, Bob Marley's song "Three Little Birds" is a sweet, inspirational tune. When something happens that bothers me, singing the lyrics *Don't worry about a thing, 'cause every little thing is gonna be alright*" to myself always improves my mood.

Journal Exercise

Brainstorm some examples of phrases you could say to yourself when you need to short-circuit a negative thought.

If you had to choose a single all-purpose saying as your "feel-better-about-life mantra", what would it be?

Which songs instantly change your mood and lift your spirits when you hear them?

POSITIVE AFFIRMATIONS

An affirmation is a positive statement that you declare to be true. It refers to an aspect of your life that you would like to develop or something you would like to have happen in your life. Even though an affirmation is future-oriented (because it hasn't occurred yet), what makes it special is that you speak or write it *as if it were currently true*. That is what gives it its power, and allows it to ripen and manifest in your life.

When you were a child, you were on the receiving end of affirmations. That is, the people around you – who didn't necessarily have your best interests at heart – gave you repeated messages, which you soaked up like a sponge. Those messages were things that people "declared to be true" about you and about life. That is why those affirmations played a role in forming your core belief system, which in turn provided the basis for your negative thinking.

Because you are now re-seeding your mind as an adult, it pays to spend time carefully crafting your affirmations. This is your chance to undo those negative messages you received as a youngster that have influenced your life and how you live it. So first, consider your intentions. What would you like to create in your life? What are important qualities you would like to possess? How would you ideally like to be in the world? What changes are important for you to make?

When you choose an affirmation that resonates with you, and then repeat it to yourself, you have the opportunity to slowly but surely change your belief system and how you think about yourself and the world.

This is a sacred time for you, as it finally has become your turn to give yourself the affirmations that you know in your soul are good for you. It's what you needed to hear when you were growing up.

And remember that very significant (but simple) rule: ***What you focus on, grows.*** Meaning, the more you can incorporate your positive affirmations into your life, the easier it will be for them to take root and flower.

Examples of affirmations:

- I am grateful for all I have in my life.
- My mistakes are valuable because I learn from them.
- I choose foods that make me feel good.
- I enjoy moving my body.
- I am open to what the world has to offer.
- I am willing to make changes in my life.
- Life's challenges help me grow.
- I enjoy challenging myself.
- I am leading a balanced life.
- I am able to roll with changes.
- I can be comfortable with uncertainty.
- I am able to listen to my body.
- I appreciate my body.
- I enjoy fresh foods.
- I deserve to be loved.
- I respect myself.
- I ask for what I need.
- I dedicate time to being creative.
- I spend quality time alone every week.
- I am committed to being kind to myself.

- I honor and accept all of my emotions
- I trust the wisdom of my body.
- I am grateful for my body.
- I am worthy of love and respect exactly as I am.
- My self-worth is independent of other people's judgments.
- I accept myself exactly as I am in this moment.
- I deserve love exactly as I am in this moment.
- I am worthy simply because I exist.
- I figure out solutions to problems.
- Knowing when to quit is a sign of wisdom.

Here are some tips to get you started on creating your own affirmations:

1. Always use the present tense, as if the affirmation were already true. ("I enjoy spending quality time with my children" instead of "I *will* enjoy spending quality time with my children.")

2. No negatives! Always use the positive form of the idea you are after. (That is, "I feel at peace" is better than "I do not feel stressed.")

3. Be specific. (It helps if your affirmation is measurable, so you'll know when you achieve it)

4. Be realistic. (You don't want your subconscious to have a reason to reject your affirmation)

5. Make your affirmations short and simple to remember. (especially if you'll be writing them down)

6. You can choose to create as many affirmations as you like, but don't overwhelm yourself.

7. Your affirmations should make you feel good inside!

The best way to ensure that affirmations sink into your subconscious is to repeat them. That is why it is helpful to create a daily ritual during which you practice your affirmations. Common times are either upon awakening or before going to bed. The important thing is to be consistent.

You can say your affirmations out loud, repeat them silently in your mind, or write them down. Some people find that stating them while looking into a mirror is particularly powerful. Others find that writing an affirmation over and over again on piece of paper is a hypnotic experience that allows it to quickly take hold.

Another idea is to incorporate your affirmations into artwork. In particular, collage is an effective medium because of all the wonderful images you can find in magazines to support your intentions. You could also write your affirmations on index cards and carry them with you, looking at them throughout the day. What is important is that you *own* your affirmations. They are the perfect antidote to negativity and will foster a positive sense of change in your life.

In the end, the more aware you are of your thought processes, the more control you will have over them. And with more control comes a sense of empowerment – you will no longer be at the mercy of negative beliefs or thoughts that compel you to engage in compulsive behavior that you will later regret. Instead of being a slave to cravings, the control you have over your mind will give you the ability to make deliberate, conscious decisions that support your growth and long-term health.

CHAPTER 9

Disarming "The Inner Critic"

Home is the place I can live with myself, without hating myself.

Peggy Lampman

Connected to negative belief systems and cognitive distortions is the "inner critic." This refers to that destructive voice in your head that offers judgmental commentary, usually on a regular basis. It puts you down, makes you feel bad about yourself, keeps you stuck. Simply put, the inner critic makes you feel like crap.

The way you can tell the difference between your inner critic voice and your irrational thinking voice is by how each one addresses you. The following are examples of irrational thinking.

"I shouldn't ask that guy out. He might turn me down."

"I'm afraid to travel abroad, since I might get sick."

"He must think I'm stupid for asking that question."

"Life never turns out the way I want it to."

"I feel guilty that I ate that food; I should've known better."

Notice that these are in the first person ("I") and third person ("he/she/it"). With irrational thinking, you will have the sense that you are truly talking to yourself, or that you are making a statement about life that is not coming from an obvious outside source (such as a parent or teacher).

You can always tell the inner critic, however, because it addresses you using the second person ("you"). It feels like there is actually someone or something else in your mind who is speaking to you with a sense of judgment. And the way your inner critic usually talks is with a strong emotional charge, such as venom, condescension, or disappointment.

"You can't do anything right!"

"You break everything you touch!"

"Who do you think you are, wanting to apply for that job?"

"See how lazy you are!"

"Wow, you really have gained a lot of weight. You look fat."

"You're an idiot for eating that! You have no self-control!"

"I can't believe you did that. What a loser."

Your inner critic is based on an outside person or thing that has taken up residence in your mind. This is what makes it so destructive – it's as if there is a parasite living inside you, draining your energy and zest for life. There are a number of different ways in which the inner critic works:

- It accepts nothing less than perfection
- It (negatively) evaluates everything you do
- It tries to control your desires and behaviors by shaming you
- It emphasizes that you are not working hard enough
- It demeans you and undermines your self-confidence by attacking your self-worth
- It attacks your fundamental right to exist
- It makes you feel guilty about things you have done in the past
- It points out – and over-emphasizes – mistakes you have made
- It pushes you to take on a role that is not natural for you (such as being a care-giver or protector)

There is hope, however! Here are four steps you can take that will assist you in neutralizing this negative force.

STEP 1

Understand who your critic is. First you must get a sense of the origin of this force that is so quick to judge you. Sometimes, this is the only step necessary for de-fanging an inner critic. This is because once you recognize your critic for who it really is, it will become easy to ignore, blow off or extinguish.

Please answer the following questions in your journal.

When you were young:

Whose approval did you value most?

Whom did you want to impress?

From whom did you want to hear the words "I value you"?

Why did you need to hear that?

Was there somebody in your life who criticized or judged you? Did it happen repeatedly or just once? What were the circumstances? How did it make you feel when it occurred?

Today:

> Whose approval do you value most?

> Whom do you want to impress?

> Is there someone in your current life who judges or criticizes you? What are the circumstances?

> From whom do you want to hear the words "I value you"?

> Why do you need to hear that?

Take some time to get a sense of who your critic is. Pay close attention to where its voice is coming from inside your body. Is it a parent? A teacher? A partner? A monster?

STEP 2

Get in touch with what your critic is telling you.

As you go through your day, notice when your critic makes an appearance. What are you doing when it speaks to you? When it does, what does it say to you? What kind of language does it use? How does it speak to you? Does it whisper? Scream? Demand? Cajole? Ridicule? What patterns are you noticing? Write your observations in your journal.

STEP 3

Recognize the rationale behind your critic.

Believe it or not, your inner critic *sometimes* has a positive intent. That is, in its own way, it is doing its best to help you avoid pain. For example, it might want to protect you from failure or rejection. Or it might want to assist you in gaining approval or attention from others. It also could be trying to prevent you from hurting yourself or being too vulnerable.

On the other hand, your inner critic may be the internalized voice of somebody close to you who said mean things to you when you were a child. Or it could be a current partner who is abusive and is trying to destory your self-esteem. No positive intent there.

Either way, it is important for you to be clear about the intention of your inner critic.

If you don't already know, the best way to find out the intention of your inner critic is to ask it directly. Here is an exercise that will allow you to do that:

Find a quiet place where you can be undisturbed. Allow yourself to become centered. You can close your eyes if you wish. Take a deep breath as you give yourself permission to access your inner critic. Have your journal and pen or pencil handy.

1. Allow you mind to soften and think back to the last time your inner critic judged you. Allow yourself to get a clear picture in your mind of how it appeared or might have appeared to you. Begin to pay attention to its details.

2. When you are ready, take a break, and give the inner critic form by drawing it in your journal. Don't worry about your skill as an artist, just try your best. Be sure to include:
    a. Its size, form, color(s), shape, and texture
    b. Any other identifying characteristics

3. Put your pen or pencil down and refocus your attention on the inner critic's presence in your body or mind. Request permission to speak with it. If you do gain permission, please ask the following questions:
    a. Where did you come from?
    b. Why do you judge me?
    c. What do you want from me?
    d. How did you help me in the past?
    e. How do you currently help me?
    f. How can you help me in the future?
    g. How do you keep me stuck?
    h. What can you teach me?

4. When you are done communicating with your critic, journal on the following:
    a. What key insights did you gain from your responses to the above questions?
    b. Were there other feelings/thoughts that came up for you as you brought form to your inner critic?
    c. Think about what made the critic so fearsome when you were younger. Are those same fears valid now that you are an adult? If this is a recently installed inner critic, you can ask yourself what makes it so frightening now? Are those fears justified?
    d. How might your insights help you move forward?

STEP 4

Decide what to do about your inner critic.

There are several ways you can deal with your inner critic. If you have discovered that your critic actually does have a positive intent, then it will be healing to dialogue with it. You can return to a conversation with your inner critic in order to negotiate or make peace with it. It is always beneficial to ask your critic what it is afraid might happen if it didn't harangue you.

For example, if your critic is a perfectionist, maybe it believes that if it didn't pick on you, then you would fail in life. So it means well; it is just going about things in a wrong-headed manner. Or a critic who is always preventing you from meeting new people is really trying to protect you from rejection.

Knowing this information will allow you to work together with your critic, so that you can encourage it to take on another, less problematic, role within your psyche. Ideally, you can thank it for caring so much about you, and then reassure it that its concerns aren't valid anymore because of the resources you now have as an adult. Then you can gently escort it to a distant corner of your psyche, where it will be out of the way. Or you and your critic can come up with other ways of looking out for you that don't involve criticizing or judging. That is, perhaps your critic can use their characteristics to assist you in a healthy, productive way.

If, on the other hand, your inner critic is the internalized voice of a parent, caregiver or partner who simply was mean, then it is a wise decision to banish or exorcise it from your psyche.

If you are in doubt about what to do with an inner critic who is nasty to you, consider this question:

> Why might you be willing to continue to internalize the voice of a person from your past who did not have your best interests at heart?

Getting rid on an inner critic is not easy, since it has lived with you for so long. But it can be done. It is necessary that you use your creativity to figure out a powerful ritual in which you can say "Good-bye." One option is to create an imaginary funeral or go through a divorce from it. You could also bury, burn, or destroy a piece of artwork that represents your inner critic. Some people find that writing a letter to their inner critic is an effective way of banishing it. Just the act of writing the letter can be healing. When it is finished, it is up to you what to do with it.

As with artwork representing the inner critic, you could do something physically to the letter in a special ritual. Or you could simply keep it in a special place.

The key is to plan and complete a ceremony with the intention of releasing the critic from its privileged place in your mind and psyche. After all, now that you are an adult you have much more power than you did when you were younger. You know now that it doesn't serve your best interests to give someone so mean-spirited a place in your life. After all, what makes your critic so special? Were they themselves perfect? What gave them the right to judge you? As Jesus so poignantly spoke (in the gospel of John) to his disciples who wanted to condemn a woman of adultery, *"Let he who is without sin throw the first stone."*

When you are able to recognize that your inner critic is not perfect and was just a person – like you – then you can tap into the courage and determination to release its grip from your soul. Ideally, the clarity you gain about your inner critic is enough to unmask and unseat it. It's like Dorothy pulling back the curtain and discovering that the Wizard is really a bumbling little man. All it takes is your intention to move in that direction.

I do, however, want to spend some time discussing how to deal with an inner critic who is a parent. This can be difficult because children often grow up with conflicting feelings:

*I love my mother. She's my **mother**! I'm supposed to love her. She's supposed to love me.*

At the same time...

She abused me. She told me she wished I'd never been born. Then she told me she loved me. I'm confused.

The first thing to do is recognize that your parent was dealing with their own issues, which influenced how they treated you. Now, this absolutely does not excuse their behavior. I want to be clear about that. If a parent abused you, physically, mentally, emotionally or sexually, then of course that was wrong. At the same time, however, it is important for you to recognize that parents often are dealing with their own demons that their children have no way of understanding. Your parent was only human, doing the best they could with what they had. In my therapy practice, I often find that abusers were themselves abused as children. Therefore, they never learned how to give and receive love in a healthy manner.

The important thing is that the pain a parent continues to inflict on you (as internalized critic) needs to end now. And that means making peace with the past. Not necessarily forgiving – that is up to you. Rather, what is healing is acknowledging that it is time to move forward because what is done is done. And honoring the fact that you survived.

You can begin to move in that direction by writing a letter to your parent-critic (even if they have passed away). Tell them how you felt growing up. Pour your emotions onto the page. Express how their criticism of you has continued to occupy space in your mind. If there was something you needed from them when you were a child, ask for it (not that you will receive it. However, just being able to ask – which you probably couldn't do when you were young – can be powerful). When you are finished with the letter, follow your intuition as to what to do with it. I favor rituals, such as burning, burying or tearing. Think about something symbolic you could do with the letter that would bring you peace about the fact that a parent has been your critic.

As you think about the role of your parent in your life, consider focusing on memories of them being kind and loving, and release the memories of them being dysfunctional and judgmental. This doesn't mean forgetting about how they treated you. Rather, it is choosing to shift your focus away from their negative hold on you. You are much more powerful now that you are an adult. Perhaps you can see that by internalizing their critical voices, you now are victimizing yourself a second time around. It was bad enough that it happened once, in real time. But the fact that you have had to carry them around as an inner critic means that you have truly suffered enough. However you choose to do so, whether with a letter or some kind of ritual, lightening your load will make a profound difference in your life.

YOUR ADVOCATE

Sometimes it is difficult to truly banish your inner critic. No matter what you do, it continues to be a presence in your mind. But please do not worry. There is an effective way to shut your inner critic down when it makes an appearance.

The key is to have a response ready the next time you are assailed by your inner critic. And that response will come from your **advocate**, whose job is to protect you from the inner critic. Your advocate is an anti-critic; it serves you by providing comfort and uplifting support. It helps you create strong, healthy boundaries that protect you from negativity. It cares deeply about you, and has your best interests at heart. No matter what, it is always in your corner. Your advocate knows you are doing the best you can – after all, nobody is perfect – and it seeks to defend you when you are being unfairly attacked by anyone, especially your inner critic.

Your advocate can appear as a person or animal. Actually, it can take any form at all, as long as it resonates with you. The important thing is that you are able to connect with its positive, affirming energy.

EXERCISE FOR FINDING YOUR ADVOCATE

Set aside some time when you won't be disturbed. Make yourself comfortable, either sitting up or laying down, but keep you journal handy. Take some deep breaths and center yourself. Closing your eyes, relax and focus on clearing your mind. As you do so, tell yourself, "I am looking for my advocate. I am looking for my protector. I am looking for someone or something that will support me and that cares for me unconditionally. I will be patient and wait for it to appear."

Let your intuition lead the way. Notice what comes into your mind's eye. See if you can get a sense of your advocate. Be patient as you notice what form coalesces in your imagination...What does it look like? What is its energy like? Does it have a message for you? What kinds of things will it say and/or do in order to challenge your inner critic? How will it defend – and encourage – you?

When you are ready, re-orient yourself and write what you experienced in your journal.

You might like to make a drawing or painting of your advocate. You can create an image of your advocate using other forms of art, such as clay or collage if you like. You could even write a poem about it.

Another option is to choose an object that represents your advocate, and carry it with you during the day. By having it close, the energy of your advocate will always be by your side.

I would like you to practice accessing your advocate during the day. Your goal is to quickly be able to utilize that imagery/energy whenever the inner critic makes an appearance. As soon as your inner critic tries to judge you, your advocate can challenge it and shut it down. This way, the inner critic can be managed, and your psyche – that part of you that is being criticized – will be protected. Your advocate can also serve as a mentorn and provide you with guidance if you need it or assist you in developing an action plan for something you'd like to undertake. It's everything your inner critic is not...

CHAPTER 10

Dealing with Cravings

Between stimulus and response there is a space. In that space is the power to choose our response. In our response lies our growth and freedom.

Viktor Frankl

The quieter you become, the more you can hear.

Ram Dass

Ordinarily we don't let ourselves experience ourselves fully. We have a fear of facing ourselves. Many people try to find a spiritual path where they do not have to face themselves but where they can still liberate themselves. In truth, that is impossible. We have to be honest with ourselves. We have to see our gut, our real shit, our most undesirable parts.

Chogyam Trungpa Rinpoche

Where you stumble, there lies your treasure.

Joseph Campbell

...and that ties in with what the Native Americans say, which is that there is always a story being told to you by every situation – and every object that you're surrounded by is telling you something if you start to look carefully.

Genesis P-Orridge

As I mentioned earlier, I define compulsions and addictions in a similar manner: Repetitive behaviors (with negative consequences) that a person cannot stop with willpower or rational thinking. Yet there are many legitimate reasons why we might be engaging in compulsive or addictive behavior:

To distract ourselves

To comfort ourselves

To sedate ourselves

To punish (ourselves and/or others)

To protect ourselves from unwanted attention (for example, weight gain)

To regulate an unbalanced biological system

To receive care-giving responses from others

To keep others at a distance

To procrastinate (that is, as a way to avoid doing something we need to do)

To give the illusion of being in control (for example, anorexia)

To self-medicate against the pain, anxiety, rage, fear, and physical distress caused by trauma

Likewise, there are a multitude of feelings and emotional/physical states that can trigger a complusion or craving:

Boredom...Loneliness...Excitement...Loneliness...Love...Frustration...Being tired...Anger...Sadness...Stress...Anxiety...Depression....Hunger...

I do believe that you can begin to heal from an addiction *if* you are willing to pay close attention to its presence in your life. The key is to avoid resisting your compulsion. Don't just force yourself to stop. Avoid willpower, because when you compete with yourself you never win. For now, I would just like you to practice noticing when you experience a craving. Be curious. Follow your compulsions. Explore and examine the feelings that lead to your urge. Those moments when you are craving something in order to deal with an emotional issue are actually quite valuable. That is because a craving indicates that there is a deep need begging to be met. In a real sense, the symptom is a messenger asking you to pay attention to some core truth or wound. It is a sacred call for self-transformation.

So whatever the reason or the trigger, I would like you to view your compulsions as a gift: a divine wake-up call, serving as a guide to show where you need look to find the pain and then to heal.

At this point, don't worry about getting rid of your compulsion or manipulating it. Your main job is working to *understand* your behavior. Your craving is a signal for you to pay attention to your emotional truth. Accordingly, an addiction has a deep, compelling personal meaning for each person. What is most important is for you to be kind to yourself and to refrain from judging yourself. After all, if you had a more compelling healthier alternative for dealing with emotions, you'd already be utilizing it!

Instead, be open to the message that your compulsion is sending. Only then is change possible. I believe that very often at the bottom of a person's addiction, there is pain. Discovering and engaging with that pain will allow a person to resolve what needs to be resolved, and thereby end the need for the compulsion.

To begin, let's explore the beginnings of your compulsive behavior. Please answer the following questins in your journal.

1. What are your first memories of engaging in your compulsion?
2. Did you learn how to use it in that way on your own, or from somebody else?
3. Currently, what does your compulsion do for you that is valued or needed in your world?
4. To what problem is your compulsion a solution, or an attempt at a solution?
5. How has your compulsion been an actual success for you, rather than a failure?
6. What do you think would happen if you stopped engaging in your compulsion?

Please complete the following:

- I engage in _____ (my compulsion) for this specific purpose:

Based on what you just wrote, would you agree with the following sentence? Why or why not?

- "For me, achieving this purpose is worth the specific pain and troubles that accompany this compulsion."

NOTICING PATTERNS

One way to begin understanding your compulsion and the roots of your cravings is to keep a diary. Doing so will help you discover the links between when and why you are engaging in your compulsion. As the days go by, it will be interesting (and illuminating) for you to notice what patterns emerge. Your diary can be a powerful tool, because it will force you to slow down and really think about your habits.

Once you are able to clearly understand when and why you are engaging in your addiction the way you do, you will b able to figure out effective strategies for addressing habits that you'd like to change.

You can keep your diary in any kind of notebook, large or small. You could also use a digital device like a computer, tablet or smartphone if that is easier. Just make sure it is convenient for you to carry around and write in.

In your diary record the following information:

1. Time of day and location
2. Your mood (and why you are in that mood)
3. What you did (in terms of your compulsion)
4. How much of it you did
5. How you felt during your compulsive behavior
6. How you felt afterwards
    a. Physically
    b. Emotionally

Keep your diary for at least two weeks. This is not necessarily a time of change for you. Rather it is one of exploration. So be curious and be patient. When you are ready to change, you will! In the next section, you will learn what to do when you are ready to address your cravings.

MANAGING CRAVINGS

Urges behave like waves – they start small, build to a crest, then break up and dissolve. When you urge surf, you ride the wave rather than fight it; as a result, you are less likely to be pulled in or wiped out.

Susan Nolen-Hoeksema

When you find yourself seeking to engage in compulsive behavior, it is time to use your mindfulness skills. Awareness is the key that will help you figure out what is initiating your desire to engage in a compulsive behavior. This is when I would like you to take a step back and observe (non-judgmentally) the emotion you are feeling and then describe it to yourself.

"I am starting to get angry." "I feel sad." "I am lonely." "My stress is beginning to overwhelm me." "I'm bored and just have no idea what to do with myself." "I'm really excited about my date."

Next, utilize your positive self-talk as you have a conversation with yourself, starting with the questions: "Will engaging in this behavior really help me deal with this feeling?" and "Will this compulsion get me closer to what I really want or will it separate me?"

The dialogue you have with yourself as you witness your urge to engage in a complusion is important, as it will influence your ability to discard this behavior and move in a healthier direction.

As you continue to notice your urge to engage in a compulsion, ask yourself:

1. What am I aware of, right now?
       a. What thoughts are going through my mind?
       b. What am I feeling?

2. What do I need, right now?

3. How am I stopping myself from getting it, right now?

This is the time to remember the skills you have learned in previous chapters. When you are connected with your core values and able to tap into your self-compassion, it becomes easier to turn away from going down a path that you know won't serve your interests.

I particularly like the SIFT system developed by author M.J. Ryan, which will allow you to strengthen your "witness self." As you notice your compulsive urges, give yourself permission to take a step back. Take a breath and then ask yourself the following questions. They will cause a rupture in your "trance" and allow you to see your situation in a different light.

1. **S**ensations: What are the sensations in my body? (heat, cold, pressure, constriction, expansion) Where are they located?

2. **I**mages: What images are coming up?

3. **F**eelings: What emotions am I experiencing?

4. **T**hinking: What are the stories I am telling myself?

You can use the SIFT method with any kind of compulsion in order to gain enough time to **pause** before you do something you regret. This time-out is something that most people skip when they are experiencing a craving. They just move from having a certain feeling to developing a compulsion to engaging in the behavior. It's like having tunnel-vision or being in a trance, with no distractions getting in the way of the craving!

So what will allow you to break the trance? Your mindfulness and self-talk skills, coupled with your self-compassion, curiosity and connection with your core values.

When you notice you are having a craving, that is the exact time to tell yourself: "I'm aware I'm having a craving. But what's really going on? I guess now I have a moment of decision. Am I going to go down this path? Or am I going to turn away and walk down another path?"

With practice, you will come to understand the moment of craving as an important crossroads. For you already know where one path leads; you've been down it many times before. It seems to make sense in the moment, but it truly never leads anywhere. In fact, it seems to go in a circle, leading back to where you came each time, only with extra regret. The other road, however, keeps going forward. It may be unfamiliar to you right now, and while challenging, it does eventually lead to healing and peace. Might you be willing to give it a chance?

Taking control of a compulsion begins when you recognize what is happening and why. That conscious moment of decision, **before** you act on your craving, is the moment of possibility. Your goal must be to fully inhabit that moment, and, if possible, stretch it out so that you can act with deliberation instead of flipping on your tunnel vision and going into the trance that leads you somewhere you truly don't want to go. In the end, the fact that you recognize that you have a **choice** about what to do about your emotions is what will give you the power to break the apparent monopoly of your compulsion or addiction.

But for this to work, you first must be able to understand what you're truly needing in that moment, and then have the ability to get that need met in a healthy way. Earlier in this book you learned about developing self-compassion and honoring your needs and how to meet them. Those are the skills that will enable you to make new choices in that moment of decision before you act on an urge.

It is also true, however, that most people haven't had the opportunity to learn how to manage difficult emotions. And because those emotions are often at the root of our addictions, that skill is essential to breaking this habit. In the next chapter I will discuss how to handle feelings in a healthy way. For right now, I would just like to focus on using your inner dialogue to help you to learn more about why your cravings are coming up in the first place.

Besides using SIFT, when you are having the urge to engage in compulsive behavior, you could ask yourself these additional questions in order to gain clarity about your situation.

- What's going on here with this urge?
- Am I being honest with myself?
- How is my compulsion promising to give me relief? Will it really?
- What's been my experience using this kind of behavior in the past to find relief?
- What's really bothering me? Why am I feeling this way?
- Could I just allow this feeling to be here without reacting to it? What gets in the way of doing that?
- What do I really need in this moment?
- What is preventing me from getting that need met?
- What can I do in the future to address that need?
- What can I do right now other than ---?

I hope that the feedback you have gotten from this workbook is allowing you to gain a deeper understanding of your why you might engage in complusive behavior and how that process works in your life. Perhaps that awareness will lead you to discard this habit. However, if you are not yet ready to give up compulsion, that is fine. After all, until you find better ways of managing emotions, it makes sense to continue to use it as a coping tool. The key is to remain mindful of what you are doing and why. This is because resisting a habit you are not ready to change will only make it stronger. So please don't feel guilty about engaging in your addiction! After all, if you had a healthier way to cope, you would use it. I believe that when you are ready, you will change.

I do wonder, though, how engaging in compulsive behavior to manage your emotions would change if you decided to do it with your full, undivided attention. What might you notice?

COMPULSION AS SPIRITUAL PRACTICE

What if you decided to make engaging in your compulsion:

- A meditation?
- A ceremony?
- A beautiful experience?
- A chance to honor a "bad habit"?
- An exercise in curiosity?
- An opportunity to be self-compassionate?

Yes, I am actually asking your "honor" your compulsive habit and show it some respect! Since you're going to engage in it anyway, why not own the experience? Think of this as a chance to truly inhabit your addictive behavior, in order to learn how it truly affects you.

For example, let's say your compulsion is emotional eating. The next time you feel a craving, please do the following:

- Sit down and make yourself comfortable
- Acknowledge the fact that you are eating to deal with an emotion
- Forgive yourself, and then give yourself permission to eat
- Focus on what you are doing
- Go slowly and deliberately
- Be conscious of what you are doing
- Divide the process of preparing your food and eating into as many small acts as possible
- Pay attention to each step of your emotional eating experience.

o Also pay close attention to each bite and how it affects you, both physically and emotionally.

While you are eating, you can ask yourself:

o What kind of relief am I experiencing?
o Does this feel like **love**? (If not, what does it feel like?)

After you are done eating please remember to treat yourself with kindness and compassion. As I said above: At this point, emotional eating might be your best coping tool for emotions and stress. And that's OK. When you find healthier, more empowering ways of coping, you will change. So acknowledge that you are doing the best that you can right now. That means no guilt or remorse! Also, please do not deprive yourself of food the next day in order to make up for what you ate.

Remember that engaging in a compulsion is never wasted time if you can learn from it. Therefore, it might be helpful to take some time to journal about your experience with, in this case, "mindful" emotional eating.

- How was this experience with emotional eating different than my prior experiences doing it?
- What did I learn about my habit?
- What did I learn about myself?

***

My hope is that you now understand your compulsive behavior much better than you did before. Since you know that your compulsion does not serve your interests in the long run, perhaps you are truly ready to leave it behind. Now your next step is to discover alternative coping strategies for managing difficult emotions. That is the purpose of the next chapter.

CHAPTER 11

Managing Emotions

There seems to be some connection between the places we have disowned inside ourselves and the key to where we need to go. Life as usual has arranged a way in which we're not allowed to leave anything behind that is not somehow resolved.

David Whyte

The only way to live an authentic life is to explore, acknowledge, and embrace the dark aspects of your soul that compel you to make choices that generate pain and hardship.

David Simon

Every moment you are being born anew. Every moment you die, and every moment you are born. Tremendous changes happen every day. It is a flux. Everything goes on flowing, nothing is frozen. But the mind is a dead thing, it is a frozen phenomenon. If you act from the frozen mind, you live a dead life. You don't live really – you are already in the grave. Drop reactions. Allow more and more responses. To be responsive is to be responsible. To be responsive, to be responding, is to be sensitive. But sensitive to here and now.

Osho

Consider the following four scenarios:

1. Jane is using a hammer as she repairs her fence. She bangs her thumb. She immediately thinks to herself, "I can't believe I just did that. I'm such an idiot." Even though nobody is around, she turns red and gets angry at herself. Continuing to berate herself as she rubs her thumb, she begins to feel depressed and ends up going inside, where she serves herself a big bowl of cereal.

2. Every Wednesday evening Larry's sister Wendy calls him. Wendy has a chronic illness and has been calling Larry regularly for over a year in order to vent. Larry generally doesn't speak much during these conversations, which last about an hour. Larry finds that on Wednesdays he feels out of sorts and usually doesn't have much of an appetite for dinner.

3. John is a teacher. It's the last day of classes before summer break. He thinks about how much he's going to miss his students. This makes him feel sad. On the way home he stops at the store to pick up a box of cookies. He knows they'll make him feel better.

4. Laura's father passed away when she was ten years old. At the funeral Laura wanted to cry but her mother put her hand on her shoulder and said, "Big girls don't cry. Let's be strong, now." For her mother's sake, Laura stifled her tears. Today, as an adult, Laura finds it difficult to respond emotionally when something sad happens. However, she does notice that every so often – apparently at random – she'll feel a heavy sense of sadness wash over her. This disturbs her, so when it happens she distracts herself by scrolling through her Facebook account.

In this chapter, I would like to discuss how to handle feelings and emotions (I will be using these two terms interchangeably) in a healthy way. After all, there has to be a compelling alternative if you're going to stop using an addiction or compulsion to deal with unwanted feelings. There has to be *something* you can do that you won't regret afterwards.

I began with the above scenarios because it is important to recognize that not all emotional landscapes are the same. This means that there will be different strategies for handling emotions, depending on their context. As you will see, some emotions deserve to be honored. Others, not so much.

My goal is for you to be able to understand the place of emotions in your life so that you can **respond** to them appropriately instead of **react** to them in ways that are not in your best interests. The key skill that makes all the difference in navigating your emotions is mindfulness. For with awareness comes the power to make positive changes. In addition, being able to step into witness consciousness will give you the necessary distance to recognize your internal processes without being completely subsumed by them.

FIRST SCENARIO

> Jane is using a hammer as she repairs her fence. She bangs her thumb. She immediately thinks to herself, "I can't believe I just did that. I'm such an idiot." Even though nobody is around, she turns red and gets angry at herself. Continuing to berate herself as she rubs her thumb, she begins to feel depressed and ends up going inside, where she serves herself a big bowl of cereal.

This is a common occurrence for all of us. Look at the following sequence of events:

1. Something happens out of the blue.
2. Your negative thinking or inner critic kicks into gear.
3. You begin experiencing distressing emotions.

As you go throughout your day, random events happen that affect you emotionally. Lousy service at a restaurant. A driver who cuts you off. A friend who doesn't respond to your text. When these things happen, you tell yourself things about the situation that then lead you to feel a certain way.

SOLUTION

You will be able to diffuse your distressing emotions by using the skills you learned earlier in the book that focused on negative self-talk and your inner critic. After all, these kinds of feelings are based on cognitive distortions or your inner critic's monologue. Taking a step back (utilizing your witness consciousness) will give you the opportunity to challenge the voices in your head that are causing your negative feelings. This is also a good time to make use of your positive affirmations or a mantra. "Oh, well – nobody said life is fair." "All I can do is try my best." "I'm not going to let this ruin my day." "I'm not going to let some jerk control my mood."

Once you challenge your negative thinking or shut down your inner critic, the emotion should dissipate on its own. As you breathe deeply you will notice how it feels to release the negativity. Then you can shift your focus to something else and move on.

The Serenity Prayer is another handy tool that can put things in perspective for you:

God, grant me the serenity

To accept the things I cannot change,

Courage to change the things I can,

And the wisdom to know the difference.

Because no matter how hard you wish you hadn't banged your finger with a hammer, the fact is you did. It's over. So now the choice is either to add a layer of suffering over the pain by continuing to ruminate over what happened. Or to take a deep breath, make a mental note to pay more attention to what you're doing, and get on with your project.

SECOND SCENARIO

> Every Wednesday evening Larry's sister Wendy calls him. Wendy has a chronic illness and has been calling Larry regularly for over a year in order to vent. Larry generally doesn't speak much during these conversations, which last about an hour. Larry finds that after these phone conversations he feels irritable and frustrated. He usually doesn't have much of an appetite for dinner and goes to bed feeling out of sorts.

This is a situation in which feelings are **legitimately** arising in response to an issue that needs to be resolved. That is, instead of being driven by irrational thinking, Larry's feelings are a natural consequence of what he is experiencing. In this case, his feelings are important feedback, telling Larry that something needs to change about the situation. It's as if the feelings are a big red flag, signaling that something isn't right about what is happening.

Another example would be a wife getting angry because her husband doesn't call her when he stays late at the office. Sitting at home alone waiting, she finds it all too easy to have a sugary snack. In this instance, the wife's need to feel like her husband cares enough to phone is not being met, which then naturally leads to anger and frustration.

Fortunately, there are several ways to address these kinds of situations so that they do not provoke distressing feelings.

SOLUTION

First, it is necessary to recognize the connection between negative feelings and the situation that is generating them. Because negative feelings often lead to cravings and compulsive behavior, keeping a diary will allow you to easily see these patterns. Next, instead of ignoring those feelings or distracting yourself with a compulsion, it will be important to spend some time being present with those feelings. They are your allies begging you to pay attention to what is going on. So journaling about them or simply noticing how they unfold will force you to take a closer look at the situation. As you do so, you can contemplate the following important questions:

1. Am I giving away any of my personal power in this situation? How so?

2. How are my boundaries? Is there something I am tolerating or allowing that is not in my best interests?

3. Is this a situation I have any control over? If I do not, how can I change my perspective so that I may make peace with it? If I do have some measure of control, then what is preventing me from getting my needs met? What can I do to strengthen my resolve to change the situation? Is there somebody or something I can use for support?

4. Where does my responsibility lie in creating and/or maintaining this situation?

If you are having trouble with your boundaries and sticking up for yourself, then it will be helpful for you to return to the chapters on self-compassion and combating negative belief systems and self-talk. This is because when you care deeply about yourself, you won't allow another person to take advantage of you or put you in an uncomfortable situation. You will know that you are worthy of respect and that it is OK to ask that your needs be met. In addition, it will be important for you to address any negative internal dialogue that is preventing you from asserting yourself.

If you find that you have little or no control over the situation (you hate your boss but still have to take meetings with him), then the key is to prepare in advance to manage your negative emotions. After all, this will be something you can predict. So after the distressing situation occurs, you could arrange things so that you are able to:

1. Go exercise
2. Have a nice meal
3. Spend time with friends or family, to whom you can vent

4. Take a drive and listen to your favorite music
5. Read an inspiring book (some people like to look at a passage from the Bible)
6. Take a kick-boxing class
7. Journal
8. Clean your house
9. Garden

It doesn't matter what you do, as long as you can distract yourself from ruminating on negative thoughts and sinking into negative feelings. Some people find that organizing something (their office, kitchen, garage) can be helpful because it gives them a sense of control and satisfaction. Another great tool to use in these kinds of situations is the *Emotional Freedom Technique*, which I will describe below. And one additional thing to consider is volunteering. Assisting people or caring for animals is an easy way to redirect attention and generate positive feelings.

According to the old Chinese proverb:

If you want happiness for an hour, take a nap.

If you want happiness for a day, go fishing.

If you want happiness for a year, inherit a fortune.

If you want happiness for a lifetime, help somebody.

THIRD SCENARIO

John is a teacher. It's the last day of classes before summer break. He thinks about how much he's going to miss his students. This makes him feel sad. On the way home he stops at the store to pick up a box of cookies. He knows they'll make him feel better.

In cases like this, something happens that legitimately leads to an emotional reaction. Neither cognitive distortions nor the inner critic play a role here. Nor is the situation a reminder of some past event or an indication that something currently is wrong and thus needs to be changed. Instead, you are simply responding to an event or situation in the present that naturally causes you to feel one or more emotions. Watching a sad movie. Moving from a childhood home. Hearing a piece of bad news. Learning about an injustice in the world. Accidentally forgetting to do something you promised for a friend. Grieving the loss of somebody close to you.

Unfortunately, many of us do not attend to our emotions during these kinds of situations. What do we do instead? Avoid them, deny them, repress them, ignore them…We'll typically do anything so that we won't have to experience a distressing feeling!

It is ironic, however. Even though we often are afraid of being fully present with a feeling, the feeling itself does not have the power to kill us. On the other hand, what we often do to avoid a feeling can cause us great physical and mental harm – and even lead to death. Consider: Drinking alcohol, smoking, drugging, eating, watching TV, staying on the computer for hours at a time…..Each one is a way to distract ourselves when we want to avoid dealing with a feeling. But unless we are willing to be present with our feelings and work through them, they will stay inside of us causing problems of one kind or another. For if you deny an emotion, you then miss an opportunity to learn what is preventing you from expressing it – and thus aren't able to face a core issue that needs addressing.

SOLUTION

The key is to *feel* feelings – not avoid them. Emotions are not the enemy! They are natural forms of energy that have been triggered for some reason or another. It is important that you pay attention to your emotions and figure out what to do about them. So no more pretending they aren't there! Instead, I would like you to give yourself permission to own what you're feeling. It is OK to feel sad. It is OK to feel bitter. Or frustrated. Or angry. Or lost. Or happy. It is OK.

By embracing and fully experiencing your feelings, you then gain the power to release them in a healthy way.

My belief is that if you are having a feeling (not based on a cognitive distortion or inner critic), then it is legitimate. That is, if you are feeling something, then it deserves your attention – and should not be ignored. Like water seeking the lowest ground level, emotions also seek expression by moving through you (specifically, by leaving your body). It is an irony that when you fight against feeling a negative emotion, you actually make it stronger by denying the physical energetic release out of your body which it needs.

Emotions have a natural flow and ebb. You can see that in action by watching a very young child. It is striking how a little one can fully inhabit an emotion like anger or sadness, express it with their whole body, and then move on like nothing had happened. Unfortunately, as we grow up we often learn to either ignore our feelings or do something that interferes with them (such as eat). Instead of letting an emotion pass through us like an ocean wave, we block its natural course. And as you can imagine, damming something that doesn't want to be hemmed in takes a tremendous amount of physical and soul energy. Therefore, the challenge is to regain that initial sense of freedom when it comes to expressing emotions. Not that you should scream or wail like a three year old. Instead, figure out something to do with your emotion that gives it full expression and resolution in a way that is meaningful to you. How to do so? **It is my belief that our intuition always knows what we should be doing with our feelings. The key is to listen to our intuition and have the courage to follow it.**

So what might happen if you simply committed to be present with an emotion? You might discover that you actually become empowered when you surrender to the moment, face your feeling and then follow its lead. This is because a feeling will take you deeper into the knowledge of yourself as for as long as you remain present with it. If you allow it to direct you to where it wants you to go, then you will discover exactly what you must do to resolve it in a healthy way.

It is also significant that when you remain present with a distressing feeling, you will discover that its discomfort is cyclical, not linear. So as much as you may fear it, the feeling will not last forever! You'll find that after a difficult emotion washes over you, it gently begins to recede. It is similar to the waves of the ocean. The feeling approaches. It gathers steam. It crests. It changes. It dissolves.

This process may take some time – hours or even days. But that is OK, because by simply being present with the ebb and flow, you will notice that what the feeling is asking of you is that you be witness to it. **That you honor it by simply feeling it.** Be certain, however, that your mind stays out of the way. Negative thinking is something that can disrupt the natural flow of a feeling. Being upset over being angry or sad is certain to keep the feelings from resolving on their own.

But as I mentioned, if you have the faith to follow your intuition then you'll know what to do with a difficult feeling. Whether you scream, cry, journal, create a memorial, tear something up, or recite the Serenity Prayer – you'll know you're on the right track because you'll notice a sense of peace in your heart.

As you try to tune into your intuition, one of your biggest challenges will be the voice (either from you or others around you) that says to you, "You shouldn't be having this feeling." Or, equally as bad, "Shouldn't you be over this feeling by now?" Those are insidious lines of reasoning. As you remain present with an emotion, you will discover that it will resolve in its own time, not according to some predetermined schedule. Grief is a good example of this. For some people grieving can last for weeks. For others, it can take months and even years. Because each person is different, it is important to allow feelings to manifest and resolve in their own time. This will require your patience and willingness to treat yourself kindly as you remain present with difficult feelings. Often, just telling yourself that you are not going to rush a feeling away is enough to make it bearable and will lead to its dissolution.

When you decide to become present with a feeling, here are some suggestions of what to do:

- o Sit with it and observe how it feels within you. Just breathe, and allow yourself to be present with your emotion. Be curious about it as it unfolds and transforms itself. That's all you need to do.

- o Take a walk and see what you notice.

- o Dialogue with it out loud or in your journal.

- o Write a letter to it.

- o Free-write about it in your journal.

- o Write a poem about it.

- o Represent it in art (drawing, painting, collage, etc.).

A final suggestion. I have found that the following questions can help to turn a negative situation into an opportunity for self-growth. When something bad happens to you, be sure to embrace your feelings instead of avoiding them. But at the same time, ask yourself:

What am I learning from this?

What is this preparing me for?

Where does my responsibility lie in all this?

How is this situation giving me an opportunity to face something I have been avoiding?

As you answer each of these questions, notice what happens to the emotion(s) you are feeling.

FOURTH SCENARIO

Laura's father passed away when she was ten years old. At the funeral Laura wanted to cry, but her mother put her hand on her shoulder and told her, "Big girls don't cry. Let's be strong, now." For her mother's sake, Laura stifled her tears. Today, as an adult, Laura finds it difficult to respond emotionally when something sad happens. However, she does notice that every so often – especially when she sees a young girl with a father – she'll feel a heavy sense of sadness wash over her. This disturbs her, so when it happens she distracts herself by scrolling through her Facebook account.

This scenario involves an emotion that arises because something or someone in the present reminds you of a past situation. In psychology we call that reminder – whether it's a person, place or thing – a "trigger."

Now, it is natural to feel emotions when something causes you to recall a powerful memory from your past. For example, driving by the old house you grew up in and remembering how sad you were when you moved. Or eating Thai food and wistfully recalling your experiences in that country. The issue here is the degree to which you feel the emotions, and whether there is any lingering baggage you are still dragging around in your subconscious.

When we become triggered by something that is still unresolved, we instantly feel strong emotions. Our ability to respond to a situation is thus negatively impacted because we feel overwhelmed. This is known as reactive behavior: we are reacting to the present as if we were still in the past. This means we lose our spontaneity and can't respond to the situation in an appropriate manner. Instead, we might fly off the handle, shut down, or become very depressed. In Laura's case, when her adult self encounters something that should make her feel sad, she is reminded (subconsciously) of how she was shut down by her mother during her father's funeral. She is still hearing those words, "Don't cry..." And so she continues to be shut down. On the other hand, seeing a girl with a father triggers those feelings of sadness that have been waiting to be released since the funeral of her own father.

The important thing to remember is that triggers hold us hostage in the present by keeping us chained to our past. However, it is also true that triggers are a goldmine of information and should be respected, because they are telling us about emotional issues that we still need to address and put to rest.

SOLUTION

When something from the past (that has been resolved) brings up strong emotions in the present, it is helpful to simply be present with your feelings and let them naturally unfold. Therefore, following the solutions for scenario 3 will be most helpful. For example, if you get sad every year on the anniversary of a parent's death, then it is best to honor those feelings in a way that intuitively feels right.

On the other hand, when it comes to dealing with emotions that arise from unresolved issues from the past it is best to use your mindfulness skills to recognize what is happening to you as it is occurring. By becoming aware that you have been triggered, you can pause and give yourself a time out. And then immediately tell yourself:

"This is just a reminder of the past. That was then, and this is now. Even though this memory makes me **feel** upset, it's not **actually** occurring again right now."

The following are helpful questions that will allow you to gain control over your emotions when something in the present reminds you of a past event:

- o   What am I feeling?
- o   What does this remind me of?
- o   What do I need right now?
- o   What can I actually do about the situation?

Next, it will be important to give yourself permission to be open to your feelings. Observe them. Bear witness. Many people have been taught that they shouldn't feel certain feelings. For example, a little boy might have learned that crying is only for sissies. Or a girl's mother might have stressed "keeping it together" at family funerals. Or perhaps a child grew up in a family where anger simply wasn't done (at least out in the open).

The key is to turn towards your feelings, to be attentive to them. If you are willing to acknowledge a particular feeling fully and completely, then you will be able to give it what it wants – *recognition*. And once you recognize a feeling, you will also receive feedback from it, as far as how it needs to be expressed or resolved.

But what gets in the way of embracing a feeling?

Fear.

Those voices in your head or beliefs in your heart that push you away from discomfort, telling you that painful things will happen if you are present with your feelings:

- Once you start crying, you'll never stop.

- You're being unreasonable about things.

- You shouldn't be having this feeling, anyway.

- The hurt will be unbearable.

- The truth about the matter is just too much to handle.

Your challenge is to dispute those suppositions. For that is all they are: negative ideas about "reality" that actually are not real. I can't tell you how many people I've worked with in therapy who were afraid that they wouldn't stop crying once they started. And each was truly surprised to learn that eventually they did stop crying – and felt better for the experience.

So once again, this is where the skills you learned in the chapters about negative belief systems, negative thinking, and the inner critic will come in handy. You'll need to have a conversation with yourself in which you argue against the voice that wants the easy way out. Your response must be: "This supposed easy way out (like using food to pull my attention elsewhere) doesn't work! All it does is make me feel lousy afterwards. I'm going to take chance and do something different for a change."

Here are some detailed questions you can ask yourself if you decide to write about an emotion in your journal:

- The times when I usually experience this feeling:

- The way I usually deal with this feeling:

- The place in my body where this feeling lives:

- If this feeling had a color, it would be:

    o Shape:

    o Size:

    o Texture:

    o Temperature:

- If this feeling could talk, it would say:

- What I want to say back to this feeling:

- I block myself from knowing more about this feeling because:

- I am afraid that if I let myself truly feel this feeling, I would:
- How I would like to ideally deal with this feeling:
- A way I could use this feeling productively:
- The three things I am willing to do, starting now, to change my relationship to this feeling are:
- As I work on exploring this feeling, I will ask for support from:

When you are ready, you can also do this same exercise for other feelings that you've had a difficult time fully expressing.

WHAT TO DO NEXT

As you already know, journaling is a powerful way to heal from a painful past experience that continues to haunt you. Is there something from earlier in your life that continues to haunt you? Is there some memory that continues to carry a negative emotional charge? Is there something painful from your past that is still unresolved?

If so, please answer the following questions in your journal.

- How has this event shaped my life?
- What does this mean within my larger life story?
- How is this part of my journey?
- How might this negative event be the basis for some kind of contribution I might make to the world?
- How might it allow me to deepen my relationships to myself and others?
- How might this negative event now lead me to show myself and others more compassion?
- How has this painful event made me a more sensitive person?

In the end, your intuition will lead you where you must go in order to heal. The skills you have learned in this book will provide you with the faith, courage, and ability to simply listen to your heart and do what you know you need to do.

TAPPING

Another tool you can use to address a distressing emotion is something called *Emotional Freedom Technique* (abbreviated as "EFT"). Originally developed by Gary Craig, EFT is a form of energy psychology that is based on Chinese medicine. It uses light tapping with your fingertips to stimulate traditional acupuncture points on your face and body. By combining this physical tapping with affirmations about an emotional issue, a person can dislodge stuck energy and dissipate painful emotions. This is an easily learned, portable technique that you can use anywhere, anytime.

There is a storehouse of free information about how to do EFT on the internet. All you have to do is google "EFT protocols" and go from there. What I would like to offer you here is a basic overview. This will be enough to allow you to begin using EFT immediately to address distressing emotions.

If you find that this tool resonates with you and provides relief, then I wholeheartedly encourage you to learn more about it. EFT is something I use all the time both personally and professionally, and I am happy to be able to share it with you.

STEP 1

You can use EFT with anything that is causing you distress. This includes emotions, cravings, or even physical symptoms. To begin, think about what you are experiencing and measure it on a scale from zero (the problem is gone) to ten (the problem at its most intense). Keep that number in the back of your mind. Being aware of this number and how it changes will give you important feedback while you do EFT.

Next, create an affirmation. The pattern of this statement is always the same:

"Even though [problem or emotion], I love and accept myself."

[NOTE: If it is impossible for you to say that you love yourself, just use the phrase: "that's Ok"]

Examples:

"Even though I feel anxious about my job interview, I love and accept myself."

"Even though I am angry at my friend because of what she said, I love and accept myself."

"Even though I feel sad about missing my friend's birthday, I love and accept myself."

"Even though I am stressed out about my job, I love and accept myself."

"Even though I feel depressed because it's the anniversary of my parent's death, I love and accept myself."

"Even though this memory of my father makes me angry, that's OK."

"Even though I am craving donuts, that's OK."

"Even though I have a headache, that's OK."

"Even though I can't fall asleep, that's OK."

You can also use EFT to address negative feelings **about** negative feelings. For instance:

"Even though I hate that I'm angry at my baby daughter for crying all night, I love and accept myself."

"Even though I feel guilty about resenting my husband, that's OK."

STEP 2

Tap on your "karate chop" point with your fingers (see the diagram below on page 153) while saying your affirmation (either out loud or in your head) three or four times. This acupressure point is located on the edge of your hand, about an inch down from where your pinky joins the palm (hence the name of this point). Use pressure that feels comfortable, neither too hard nor too light. I use my index and middle fingers for tapping, although it is also fine to use your intuition as far as determining how you would like to tap. Some people find that rubbing the EFT acupressure spots is also effective. It doesn't matter which of your hands (dominant or non-dominant) you use for tapping or rubbing.

When you are done with your karate chop point, take several deep breaths and then measure your distress from zero to ten again. Notice if the number has stayed the same, gone up or moved down. Depending on what the number is, you might want to modify the affirmation or keep it the same (more on that below).

Diagram 1: The Karate Chop Point

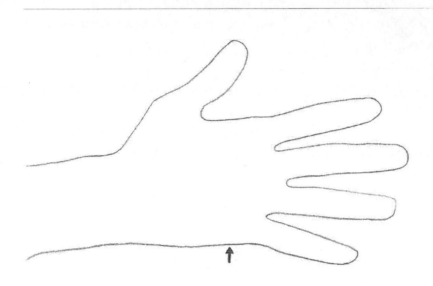

STEP 3

Now you will tap between five and ten seconds on each of the points noted on the diagram on page 156. As you do so, you will use a shortened form of your affirmation. Just use the words that describe what is bothering you. So if your affirmation was "Even though I feel overwhelmed by work, I love and accept myself," then the shortened version would simply be "feeling overwhelmed."

Other examples:

"This anger at my father"

"feeling stressed"

"this headache"

"anxiety about flying"

"Craving sweets"

As you can see from the diagram, the first point is on the crown of your head. Next, tap on your eyebrows, right above the bridge of your nose. Then move to your temples, where your eyebrows end. The next points are directly under your eyes, on the eye sockets. As the three acupuncture points around the eyes occur on each side of your face, my recommendation is to use your fingers to tap on both sides at the same time.

Next is a point on your filtrum (that little indentation right under your nose). Then you move to a point directly under your bottom lip (known as the chin point). The last two points I'd like you to tap on are known as the collar bone points. You can locate them by first feeling for your sternal notch (where the knot of a tie would go). Bring your fingertips down about an inch from that spot, and then move them away from each other about an inch. In order to ensure that you hit these points, use four fingers instead of two for tapping. The full EFT protocol includes several more points, but the abbreviated version I have provided here is a great start that has given many of my therapy clients emotional relief.

STEP 4

Congratulations! You've just completed a round of EFT. Now pay attention to how you feel. The goal is to bring your distress level to a zero. If the first round of tapping has not done that, you have two options. You could repeat the round of tapping, starting with the karate chop point, stating "Even though I **still** [have this problem], I love and accept myself." Your reminder phrase would be "still [description of problem]".

Your other option is to change the language of your initial affirmation. It could be that something else is actually causing your distress. For example, instead of focusing on your headache, it might be more fruitful to say, "Even though I am stressed about my relationship, I love and accept myself." Or, while you feel angry about getting in a fight with your son, what is also happening beneath that emotion is sadness about the situation. If that is the case you would state, "Even though I am sad that I got into a fight with my son, I love and accept myself."

Now that you have a good sense of what EFT entails, let me explain why I recommend using it. First, it is quick and convenient. You can do it anywhere, anytime. Second, it allows you to own your emotions by giving you an excuse to verbally express how you are truly feeling. Third, EFT gives you something physical to do with yourself when you are dealing with difficult emotions. So not only is it healing, but also a great distraction that will keep you from ruminating. Finally, EFT gives you the opportunity to remind yourself that even though you might be distressed by your emotions, you can still love and accept yourself.

In other words, it is OK and perfectly normal to have conflicting feelings at the same time: feeling angry at your child/loving your child/loving yourself. People often beat themselves up because they feel upset about feelings they are having, wishing the emotion wasn't present. With EFT, you can acknowledge those feelings and then immediately pair them with a positive affirmation about yourself. **Even if you don't believe the affirmation "I love and accept myself" at first, just going through the motions will begin to affect how you feel about yourself.** And as I mentioned above, if it is difficult for you to say that you love yourself, using the phrase "that's OK" is equally effective in giving you the permission to feel what you're feeling. (for example, "Even though I'm anxious, that's OK.")

If you are interested in learning more about energy psychology and feel it will be a helpful tool with your recovery, a good place to start exploring on the internet is www.eft.mercola.com

Diagram 2: EFT Tapping Points

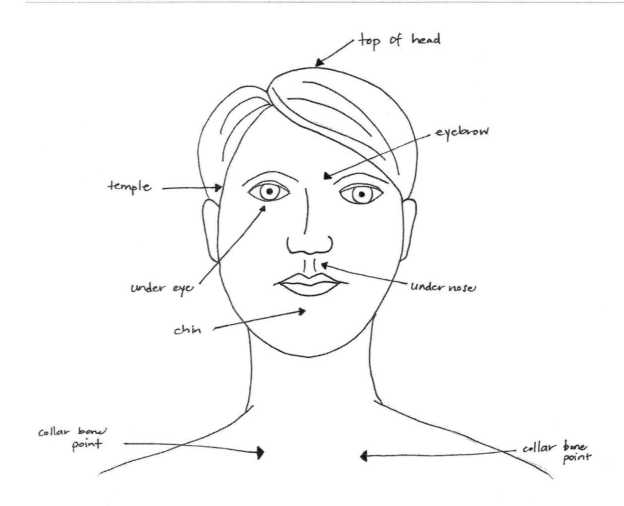

CHAPTER 12

Dealing with Stress

When I look back on all these worries, I remember the story of the old man who said on his deathbed that he had had a lot of trouble in his life, most of which had never happened.

Winston Churchill

There is more to life than increasing its speed.

Mahatma Gandhi

For fast-acting relief, try slowing down.

Lily Tomlin

The greatest weapon against stress is our ability to choose one thought over another.

William James

We live as though there aren't enough hours in the day but if we do each thing calmly and carefully we will get it done quicker and with much less stress.

Viggo Mortensen

Learn to say no to demands, requests, invitations, and activities that leave you no time for yourself. Until I learned to say no, and mean it, I was always overloaded by stress. You may feel guilty and selfish at first for guarding your down-time, but you'll soon find that you are a much nicer, more present, more productive person in each instance you do choose to say yes.

Holly Mosier

Stress can be defined as mental or emotional strain due to circumstances that feel overwhelming. When we encounter a difficult situation, our brain's sympathetic nerves send signals to the adrenal glands to release the stress hormones adrenaline and cortisol, which force our body into fight/flight/freeze mode. Ideally when the danger is over we shift back to a relaxed state and our adrenals get a rest. However, most of us spend our days stuck in stress mode, which can lead to serious physical as well as mental health problems. This is because when our body releases those stress hormones on a continual basis, almost every system in our body gets disrupted. It's like putting your foot on the gas while your car's emergency break is still engaged. Not good. And certainly not the way nature designed humans to operate.

Psychotherapists have a habit of saying "When we get stressed, we regress." That's because it's easy to revert back to old habits when we feel overwhelmed or pressured. The downside is that then we experience even MORE stress! This is why one of your strategies for recovery has to involve stress management. Without the ability to respond appropriately to stress, it will be difficult to construct a new life that feels good.

It's important that you identify the habits, behaviors, activites, people and situations that stress you out or make you feel upset. Feeling powerless about the stress in your life will only make your recovery more difficult. The good news is you have more power than you realize to handle stress. In other words, you do have options!

One of my favorite frameworks for stress management is known as the **4 A's**. You can change a stressful situation by **avoiding** it or **altering** it. On the other hand, you also have the ability to change your *reaction* to a stressor by **adapting** to it or **accepting** it.

Avoid Unnecessary Stress

You probably have more control than you think when it comes to certain stressors. For example, if there is a person in your life who stresses you out, you could avoid or limit the time you spend with them. Or if listening to the news first thing in the morning makes you upset, you could decide to take a "news fast." Perhaps the route you take to work stresses you out because of the inevitable traffic. You could always figure out an alternate route. It may be longer but at least you'll be avoiding the predictable daily frustration of sitting in your car feeling powerless.

In addition, it's important to learn how to say "no" without feeling guilty. Saying "Yes" when we really mean "No" only leads to stress and resentment. If saying "no" to a request makes you uncomfortable, figure out why. Are you afraid of conflict or disappointing someone? Are you a people-pleaser? What do you need to tell yourself to avoid feeling guilty?

All that being said, it certainly isn't healthy if you are putting off something or someone you *need* to address. (for example, breaking up with a partner or finishing a work project). In that case avoidance only creates more stress. Then your task is to explore what is behind your procrastination and figure out how to best address it.

Alter the Situation

If it's impossible to avoid a stressor another possibility is to change it. For example, perhaps it's time to be more assertive with someone who is treating you poorly. Or maybe you are unhappy with a job or relationship – but you feel stuck and believe that you have no other options ("I could never get a divorce!"). But in reality the only thing holding you back is fear (**F**alse **E**xpectations **A**ppearing **R**eal). You might think it's "impossible" to leave a job or go back to school, but the fact is that nothing is impossible; you just have to learn how to access your courage and then come up with a plan of action.

Always ask yourself, What power do I have in this situation? Is it true there is *nothing* I can do to change the situation? For example, maybe you hate getting up early when it's cold and dark in the winter. Then get a natural sunrise alarm clock, a neat gadget that gradually brightens your room as your wake up time approaches. Such a small investment can make a big difference in the quality of your life.

Adapt to the Stressor

By reframing the problem or adjusting your standards you can learn how to view a stressor with a different, more empowering perspective. In other words, if you can't change the stressor at least you change your attitude or expectations about it. For example, I hate to rush on my morning commute so to avoid feeling stressed I leave early. But I still might end up getting stuck in traffic. Since this is something I have no control over in the moment, instead of getting upset I can reframe the situation by telling myself that now I have more time to listen to music (which is something I do in the car). This internal dialogue short-circuits my anger and helps me make the best of the situation.

Another example of making the best of a situation is when a friend of mine moved to Alaska with his wife because she got her dream job at a university there. Not being a fan of the cold, he was pretty down. But since he wans't going to divorce his wife, he decided to explore all the possibilities Alaska had to offer, one of which ended up being kayaking – an activity he discovered is really fun. So even though he still isn't thrilled about the long Alaskan winters, he has no regrets about moving there because he discovered a hobby he loves. And when it's the middle of February and the nights are long and cold – and he's feeling bleak – he reminds himself that would never have gotten into kayaking if he'd never moved to Alaska. And so that reframe puts things in perspective for him in a way that reduces some of his winter suffering.

One more effective way to put things in perspective when you get upset about something is to look at the bigger picture. Because sometimes it's very easy to blow something upsetting way out of proportion. So the solution is to ask yourself: Will this matter in 10 minutes? In 10 hours? In 10 days? In 10 weeks? In 10 months? In 10 years? Is getting all stressed out really worth the energy?

Accept What You Cannot Change

Trying to control what is uncontrollable is like walking up to a wall and banging your head against it. You'll never win in a struggle against that wall of reality. Now, that doesn't mean you can't figure out what you have control over and then work on those kinds of changes (remember The Serenity Prayer?). But getting upset because the weather sucks won't change the weather.

So the last option is make peacing with what's bothering you, accepting it as it is, and moving on. Let's use being stuck in traffic again as an example. Getting angry at the cars in front of you won't get them to move more quickly. Instead of resisting the reality of what is happening and getting upset, what if you released your tension and experienced the situation as it is, not as you wished it would be? Remember, no matter how much you yell or curse, you have no control over how fast the cars in front of you are going to move. That's when you need to take a deep breath and reasses how you would like to respond to the situation you're in.

Or if you live somewhere cold but you don't want to move because you love your job. Complaining during the winter doesn't change anything – and just makes things worse. Far better to accept that coldness comes with the territory – and then do something you do have control over, which is getting your hands on the warmest long underwear you can find!

Remember, what we focus on grows, so when something upsetting happens, it's natural to get angry. But ruminating on the situation is what will throw your nervous system out of whack as you continue to pump out stress hormones. A more productive way to deal with things, once you've gotten your initial anger or disappointment out of your system, is to ask yourself two questions. "What can I learn from this?" And, "What does this make possible?"

When someone has treated you poorly, forgiveness (or at least acceptance) can go a long way to reducing your stress. That's because all of the wishing in the world won't change the past. Now, I am not advocating forgiving the perpetrators of abuse (that is something to work on with a therapist). But something to consider is that chronic anger over a situation that has already happened is a toxic emotion; it creates tension and misery that plays out physically, mentally and emotionally.

When I work with survivors of abuse and trauma, the goal is figuring out how to leave behind the resentment over what happened, because that feeling is keeping my client stuck in the past. Instead, we focus on how to create meaning out of the traumatic event(s) and what might be the best way to grieve over what was lost. We also explore what needs to happen so that my client can move forward in their lives. It's not about forgetting what happened in the past; it's about refusing to allow the past to continue to dictate one's future.

Nelson Mandela once said, "Resentment is like drinking poison and then hoping your enemies die." The only person who gets hurt in that equation is you. Again, acceptance doesn't mean that you are OK with the stressor. It means that you are acknowledging the reality of the situation and deciding that you are not going to let it control your decisions and inner life anymore. This acceptance frees up your energy so that you can investigate other options to improve the quality of your life.

***

Here are 12 more strategies and tips that will help you become resilient and better able to manage things when they don't go your way. The more you incorporate them into your life, the easier it will be to avoid stress in the first place, address it when it does occur, and bounce back afterwards.

1. Improve the quality of your sleep. Make sure you're getting 7 – 9 hours per night. Our bodies rejuvenate while we are resting, so it is important to give them a break.

2. Exercise regularly. It doesn't have to be anything fancy or even at a gym. Just a daily brisk 15 minute walk outside can do wonders.

3. Pay attention to your diet (especially stay away from sugar, caffeine and processed foods). It's a good idea to avoid consuming things that give you a burst of energy followed by an crash, so they key is to make food choices that will keep your blood sugar steady.

4. Free write each morning when you wake up or at night before bed in a journal about what's on your mind.

5. Each day do something healthy to relax.

6. Meditate. Even five minutes a day will be enough for you to begin to notice positive physiological and mental changes.

7. Practice time management. Take control of your schedule and learn the difference between "urgent" and "important."

8. Figure out what recharges your batteries. Think in terms of people, places, things and activities. Which ones give you positive energy? How can ensure that you're maximizing who or what provides you with energy, while minimizing the energy drains of your life? Remember, energy is life, so if you don't have a way to replenish yourself soon enough you'll truly be burnt out.

9. Set aside time each week to do something fun.

10. Spend time in nature.

11. Practice gratitude. During the day remind yourself what is going right for you in your life. Even if you're having a terrible day, remember that you're still breathing. And as long as you're alive, there's hope.

12. Start your day out right. Whatever you can do the night before to make sure your morning runs smoothly will pay dividends for the rest of the day.

Chapter 13

Addressing Chronic Pain

It's difficult to give up an addiction or compulsive behavior if it's helping you deal with chronic physical pain. Whether you are dependent on pain-killing medications or are using compulsive behaviors to distract yourself from the pain, failing to address this part of your life will create a major obstacle to recovery. Therefore, my goal is to help you learn how to either alleviate physical pain completely or discover how to manage it in a way that improves the quality of your life.

Some of these suggestions are things you can do on your own or with a mental health counselor. Others are done by professionals. The bottom line is that knowledge is power: the more options you have, the more likely you'll discover a way to manage your pain without having to resort to a substance or behavior that you want to give up.

At the end of the day, you must be your own advocate. You have to be proactive and search out those options that might provide relief. The guide below will get you started, but it's only the beginning. Doing a Google search for "chronic pain" plus any one of these strategies or modalities will lead you to wealth of information that you can explore. Certainly it's necessary to be skeptical. But don't let that get in the way of discovering what might very well be the key to healing from your pain.

ACCEPTANCE AND COMMITMENT THERAPY (ACT)

The philosophy behind this school of therapy is that we can learn how to accept what is beyond our control while at the same time creating a meaningful life that is aligned around our core values. ACT encourages a person to observe how they are thinking and feeling about their chronic pain without asking them to change anything. Using mindfulness skills, a person learns how to give up resistance against what they cannot change. By doing so, a person releases tension and frees up energy that can be used to pursue meaningful goals.

According to ACT, although we might not have much control over our pain, we do have the power to reduce the suffering we experience in relation to our pain. That is, it is our distress about our pain that adds a layer of suffering – which is preventable. So while living without pain might not be an option, living without suffering is.

ACT teaches a person how to discover their core values and then how to commit to and act on those values, in spite of living with pain. Living a values-driven life creates meaning and fulfillment, which ends up shifting focus away from a victim-mentality in which one's sole focus is pain management.

Recommended Books

Living Beyond Your Pain: Using Acceptance and Commitment Therapy to Ease Chronic Pain, by JoAnne Dahl and Tobias Lundgren

ACT Made Simple: An Easy-To-Read Primer on Acceptance and Commitment Therapy, by Russ Harris

ACUPUNCTURE

According to Chinese medicine, ill health is the result of an energy imbalance in the body. The key to regaining vitality is by using needles to manipulate energy that has become stuck, stagnant or sluggish so that things get moving again. Although the needles are thin and typically don't hurt, there are other ways for an acupuncturist to stimulate the necessary energy points on your body. These include using heat, magnets, pressure or electrical stimulation.

Whether or not you believe in the philosophy behind this three thousand-year-old tradition, acupuncture works for many people who suffer from chronic pain and Western scientific studies have begun validating its benefits.

Recommended Books

Acupressure for Emotional Healing: A Self-Care Guide for Trauma, Stress and Common Emotional Imbalances, by Michael Gach

Between Heaven and Earth: A Guide to Chinese Medicine, by Harriet Beinfeld and Efrem Korngold

The Web That Has No Weaver: Understanding Chinese Medicine, by Ted Kaptchuk

Wood Becomes Water: Chinese Medicine in Everyday Life, by Gail Reichstein

Healing with Whole Foods, Asian Traditions and Modern Nutrion, by Paul Pitchford

CHIROPRACTIC

Some people get nervous when they hear about chiropractors because they envision harsh spinal manipulation and back cracking. And it is true in some cases. But in my experience, it is possible to find a practitioner who is very gentle and who does very little spinal manipulation. Personally, the chiropractor I use has performed what seem to be miralces when it comes to healing back pain, so I am a fan. The key is getting good recommendations in order to find the chiropractor who is best for you.

But what exactly is chiropractic? The focus of this practice is on the musculoskeletal and nervous systems, and it addresses issues of joint functioning and pain not only in the back, but also in the head, neck and limbs. By manually adjusting joints and decreasing inflammation in tissues, a chiropractor can restore your body to a balanced, pain-free state.

COGNITIVE-BEHAVIORAL THERAPY (CBT)

The results of chronic pain can influence our behaviors (avoidance and withdrawal), emotions (anger, sadness, frustration, depression, anxiety) and thoughts (negative thinking). CBT addresses all three areas by focusing on five goals:

1. Minimizing the impact pain has on a a person's life in general

2. Assisting a person in improving how they get through the day (in terms of how they function)

3. Changing beliefs and attitudes a person has about their pain

4. Challenging irrational thinking about pain

5. Providing coping skills a person can use to manage or eliminate pain

So on the one hand, CBT is all about paying attention to self talk and limiting belief systems in order to replace them with more accurate and empowering options. When it comes to chronic pain, it's imperative to explore how we think about (and the stories we tell ourselves about):

1. The cause of our pain

2. The meaning of the pain

3. How much control we have over our pain

4. How to to treat the pain

5. What the future holds for us in terms of recovery from the pain

6. What it means to be a person who has to live with chronic pain

On the other hand, CBT also focuses on practical, concrete issues of daily living. For example some of its other main aims are helping people learn problem solving skills, sleep hygiene, time management, and how to set goals effectively.

Recommended Books

Managing Chronic Pain, by John Otis

Retrain Your Brain: Cognitive Behavioral Therapy in 7 Weeks: A Workbook for Managing Depression and Anxiety, by Seth Gillihan

Feeling Good: The New Mood Therapy, by David Burns

DEEP BREATHING

If you begin to pay attention to how you're breathing during the day, you might notice that it's a bit shallow (that is, only the top of your chest is moving when you inhale). Or you might even realize that at certain points during the day you've actually been holding your breath for an extended amount of time. And when we are experiencing pain, we often hold our breath because the pain truly takes our breath away. Or we notice that breathing in deeply increases the pain.

The problem with inhibiting our breath is that it both decreases the amount of oxygen in our blood and creates muscle tension within the body. When we develop chronic tension, those muscles never relax and therefore put pressure on other parts of our body such as bones, nerves, arteries and connective tissues.

Humans are designed to use their diaphram to breathe. This is a dome-shaped sheet of muscle that is found under the lower ribs, between the chest and stomach cavities. If you watch a baby breathe, you'll see its stomach move. That's diaphramic breathing. Unfortunatley, most of us abandon this kind of breathing around age ten and move to chest breathing, which is a lot more shallow – and therefore much less effective. In addition, moving away from diaphramic breathing means that we start using muscles in the chest, neck and jaw that weren't made for that kind of work. All of which leads to increased and chronic muscular tension – and pain.

Learning how to breathe slowly and deeply using your diaphram can have a dramatic impact on your physical and mental health. Making full use of your lung capacity allows you to take in a healthy supply of oxygen and efficiently expel waste such as carbon dioxide. This type of breathing promotes relaxation and slows respiration, both which help reduce pain. It also improves the quality of your sleep, strengthens the immune system, lowers blood pressure and increases energy levels.

To make sure you are using your diaphram to breathe, place one hand on your upper chest and the other over your belly button. When you take air in (through your nose, because your mouth wasn't made for inhalation – it dries out the air), you should feel your belly move, not your chest. And when exhaling (either through your nose or mouth) notice how your belly deflates while your chest remains stationary. This is known as belly breathing and using it is one of the quickest ways to shift how your are feeling, physically as well as mentally/emotionally.

Recommended Books

Deep Breathing Exercises for Anxiety, by Angira Lisbon

Keep Calm and Breathe, by Julie Schoen

The Healing Power of the Breath, by Richard Brown and Patricia Gerbarg

FOOD

What we eat and drink can create or exacerbate chronic pain. For example, a food intolerance is any chronic, toxic reaction to food that doesn't involve the immune system. This can be caused by different factors, such as your body not being able to fully break down or digest a certain molecule in a food. Or a food additive such as sulfite might cause a negative reaction in your gut.

There are several common nutritional culprits that could be having a negative impact on your overall state of health as well as your chronic pain.

1. Foods with tyramine or phenylalanine (derived from amino acids), which include fermented cheeses, chocolate, sausages, sour cream, red wine, avocado, beer, raspberries and yeast. People with these sensativities can suffer from migraine headaches, high blood pressure and chest pains.

2. When a person is unable to break down lactose, a sugar found in cow's milk, they have lactose intolerance. This is very common, with 1 in 4 Americans suffering from it. Symptoms include digestive distress, cramping and diarrhea, bloating and stomach pain.

3. Preservatives and additives, including food dyes, can lead to distressing physical symptoms such as hives and headaches.

4. Gluten is a name for certain proteins found in wheat, rye and barley. And unfortunately it's everywhere. Symptoms of this type of sensitivity include digestive problems, low energy, depression, anxiety, compromised immune function, migraines, skin problems, fatigue, and joint/muscle aches.

On the other hand, a food allergy is when your immune system over-reacts to a particular food, treating it as an enemy. In order to protect you, anti-bodies are released and your body creates inflammation to contain what it believes to be dangerous. When it comes to a wound, inflammation is great – it means your body doing what is necessary to heal. But chronic inflammation means that your body is continually in stress-response mode, and that leads to all kinds of negative physiological and mental effects, including pain.

According to the U.S. Centers for Disease Control, 90% of all food allergies are to one of the following:

1. Cow's milk

2. Hen's eggs

3. Peanuts

4. Soy

5. Wheat

6. Fish

7. Crustaceans (shrimp, prawns, lobster, crab)

8. Tree nuts (such as almonds, cashews, walnuts, pecans, pistachios, and chestnuts)

Research also shows that sugar causes an immune system response (i.e., inflammation), so that is also something to consider.

When it comes to chronic joint pain, a root cause for some people can be an intolerance to solanine, a naturally occuring substance found in the nightshade family of vegetables. These include eggplant, potatoes, tomatoes and peppers (bell, cayenne, chili peppers and paprikia), as well as tabacco.

Bottom line: Take a 2 or 3 week break from a specific food and notice how you feel. How are your energy levels? Your quality of sleep? Your pain? It is frustrating to discover that you have a sensitivity or allergy to a food you love. But if that is what's causing or contributing to your chronic pain, you need to know.

Recommended Books

No Grain, No Pain: A 30-Day Diet for Eliminating the Root Cause of Chronic Pain, by Peter Osborne

The Thyroid Connection: Why You Feel Tired, Brain-Fogged and Overweight – And What To Do about It, by Amy Myers

Foods That Fight Pain: Revolutionary New Strategies for Maximum Pain Relief, by Neal Barnard

The Anti-Inflammatory Diet and Action Plans: 4-Week Meal Plans to Heal the Immune System and Restore Overall Health, by Dorothy Calimeris and Sondi Bruner

GUIDED IMAGERY

In guided imagery, words and/or music are used to lead a person into an altered state of consciousness. By learning how to focus and guide their imagination, a person can experience positive changes in physical and emotional health.

The principle behind this modality is that your body will respond to mental images in the same way that it responds to real external events. For instance, what happens if I ask you to think in detail what it is like to cut up a lemon? And what if you did so while focusing in your mind's eye on the smells, sights, sounds and tactile feeling you experience while cutting into it? Odds are, your mouth will start to water. So although the lemon exists only in your imagination, your body physiologically responds as if it were actually there in front of you. In this case, mental imagery led to physical consequences.

Tension makes chronic pain worse. Any guided visualization you do that creates a state of relaxation will have a positive impact, not only on the pain itself but on the threshold of pain that you are able to endure. Guided imagery can also help with emotional distress associated with chronic pain. For example, learning how to easily access past memories of times when you felt happy or pain-free will give you a tool to use when you need to quickly change how you are feeling.

Recommended Books

Guided Imagery for Self-Healing, by Martin Rossman

Staying Well with Guided Imagery, by Belleruth Naparstek

Rituals for Healing: Using Imagery for Health and Wellness, by Jeanne Achterburg, Barbara Dossey and Leslie Kolkmeier

HERBS

As native peoples have known throughout history, there is a wide variety of plants and herbs that have pain reduction qualities. Many herbs work by reducing inflammation in the body. So while they won't address the root causes of chronic pain, plants can offer significant relief. Some more common herbs used for this purpose include ginger, turmeric, holy basil, devil's claw, arnica, bromelain and white willow bark. Certainly, before you begin incorporating herbs into your health plan, check in with your doctor.

Recommended Books

Rosemary Gladstar's Medicinal Herbs: A Beginner's Guide, by Rosemary Gladstar

Herbal Remedies: The Ultimate Guide to Herbal Remedies for Pain Relief, Stress Relief, Weight Loss and Skin Conditions, by Nicole Evans

Natural Anti-Inflammatory Remedies: A Complete Guide to Inflammation and Healing With Holistic Herbs, Diet and Supplements, by Carmen Reeves

HYPNOSIS

Have you ever gotten so lost in a book that you lost track of time? Started to cry during a movie? Didn't notice you'd been cut until you looked down and saw your leg?

These are all example of hypnosis, which occurs naturally all the time. We become so engrossed in something that we enter an altered state; distractions fade away. So one way to define hypnosis is as "focused attention." We feel relaxed, yet have a heightened level of awareness. Another characteristic of hypnosis is that while is this state, we become highly susceptible to suggestions, either from ourselves (as in self-hypnosis) or others.

Being in a hypnotic trance allows us to access parts of our unconscious that aren't normally available. It also makes it easier to communicate with and influence physical processes, such as pain. And due to our suggestibility, we can lay the groundwork for positive habit changes that will become a part of our lives long after the hypnosis session is over.

For those of you who are worried that a hypnotherapist will make you do something foolish or that you don't want to do while under (like quack like a duck), the truth is that stage hypnosis is a completely different animal. Under clinical hypnosis, you'll never do something that is at odds with your own moral code (unless you already have that desire).

Scientific studies have shown that hypnosis is effective at relieving a number of chronic pain issues, including cancer pain, low back pain, arthritis, pain associated with immune system diseases such as fibromyalgia, and headaches. Hypnosis can help you distract yourself from pain, communicate with your pain to discover its root causes, gain control over your pain, and create opportunities for you to "time travel," during which you experience pleasureable past memories of times before chronic pain entered your life.

Recommended Books

Hypnotize Yourself Out of Pain Now, by Bruce Eimer

Hypnosis for Chronic Pain Management, by Mark Jensen

Instant Sef-Hypnosis, by Forbes Blair

MASSAGE

Massage (of which there are many different types) is scientifically proven to reduce anxiety and depression. Plus it feels great. For chronic pain, massage can make a difference if you have a contracted muscle. It feels like a "knot" but what is happening is that the tightening of the muscle is restricting the flow of blood through that area of the body. In a real sense, the musicle is starving because it's not getting the supply of blood it needs to fully function. This leads to pain, not only in the muscle's location, but also in other parts of the body (this is known as "referred pain"). For example, due to networks of nerves passing throughout our bodies, a compressed muscle in an armpit can radiate pain into the forearm. This makes it easy to focus on the wrong part of the body as the origin of the pain.

Massage can be expensive, but a low-cost option is to contact a massage school near you; typically the students have to give so many hours of massages in order to graduate, which means that these sessions are discounted.

Recommended Books

The Trigger Point Therapy Workbook: Your Self-Treatment Guide for Pain Relief, by Clair Davies and Amber Davies

Trigger Point Therapy for Myofascial Pain: The Practice of Informed Touch, by Donna Finando and Steven Finando

Massage for Dummies, by Steve Capellini and Michel Van Welden

MINDFULNESS

Mindfulness focuses on the concept that pain is different than suffering. That is, we might not have a lot of control over the intrinsic quality of our pain. But we do have a great amount of control over how we respond to that pain.

Being fully present with pain – instead of staying stuck in our heads and thinking "This sucks and I wish it weren't happening" or "I hate my body" or "This is never going to end" or "This isn't fair" – changes our relationship with it. Remember: What we focus on grows, so focusing on negative thinking adds a thick layer of suffering over the pain. And that layer of suffering, that resistance to the reality of what is currently happening, makes everything worse.

So instead of hating your pain, what if you decided to adopt an attitude of curiosity about it? What if you befriended it? What if you showed your body compassion?

Instead of *reacting* with tension, frustration and anger, what if you simply decided that you would consciously *respond* to what you are feeling? You might discover that each moment is different from the rest. That when you relax and breathe into your pain...when you breathe with the pain...it actually is not a constant single sensation but rather ebbs and flows.

So changing your relationship with pain means paying attention to the thoughts and feelings you are having about it. What are you saying to yourself? Are those statements true? Are they disempowering?

Recommended Books

You Are Not Your Pain: Using Mindfulness to Relieve Pain, Reduce Stress and Restore Well-Being, by Vidyamala and Danny Penman

The Mindfulness Solution to Pain: Step-by-Step Techniques for Chronic Pain Management, by Jackie Gardner-Nix

How to Live Well With Chronic Pain and Illness: A Mindful Guide, by Toni Bernhard

Natural Pain Relief: How to Soothe and Dissolve Physical Pain with Mindfulness, by Shinzen Young

NICOTINE

There are over 4000 different chemicals in cigarettes, any number of which could be having a negative influence on your chronic pain. However, one thing is certain: the nicotine in tabacco impairs the delivery of oxygen in your blood to bones to tissues. This type of "oxygen starvation" interferes with your body's ability to regulate inflammation and makes it more difficult for your immune system to repair damage.

Recommended Book

Allen Carr's Easy Way to Stop Smoking, By Allen Carr

PAIN DIARY

Keeping detailed track of your pain in notebook or with an app might seem like the last thing you'd want to do, but it actually has advantages. Paying attention to the following variables will allow you to discover patterns and, ideally, the root causes of chronic pain that you can then address:

1. Type of pain

2. Location of pain

3. Severity of pain (from 1-10)

4. Duration of pain

5. What were you doing/thinking/feeling when it began

6. Weather

7. What, if anything, eases the pain

8. Food eaten

9. Medications taken

10. Other symptoms

Creating this kind of record usually helps you see that your chronic pain actually ebbs and flows over the course of a day/night. The key will be using the information you gather to figure out how to keep it at bay while minimizing the causes of flare-ups.

Having an accurate description of your pain will also help you communicate more effectively with doctors and other healing professionals. Here is a list of words as examples so you can better describe what the pain feels like:

Pulsing / sharp /shooting / splitting / stinging / tingling / aching / tender / tight / throbbing / cutting / burning / knot-like / pounding / cramping / pressing / prickly / numb / tugging / squeezing / deep / on the surface / pinching / sore / jumping / intermittent / nagging....

You get the idea.

While a notebook is perfect, you can also use an app on your phone for convenience. Some popular ones are:

1. Manage My Pain (Lite and Pro)

2. My Pain Diary: Chronic Pain and Symptom Tracker

3. WebMD Pain Coach

4. CatchMyPain

SLEEP

It's a vicious cycle: Pain interferes with sleep, and poor sleep exacerbates pain. Here are some tips to help you get more rest at night:

1. Use your bedroom for sleep and sex – nothing else. Reading, watching television, using the computer or phone: all done elsewhere.

2. Only go to bed when you're sleepy. If you're in bed and having a difficult time falling asleep, don't just lay there. Get up and do something else out of the bedroom. Come back when you're tired and yawning.

3. Set a consistent wake-up time and stick to it (regardless of when you go to bed).

4. Exercise improves sleep quality and quantity, but don't do it 2-3 hours before bedtime.

5. Keep your bedroom quiet, dark and cool.

6. Avoid stimulating activity and stressful situations before bed (for example,

maybe not a good idea to watch the news).

7. Reduce or eliminate caffeine.

8. Limit alcohol (it can make you sleepy but negatively impacts the quality of your sleep).

9. Practice some form of mindfulness meditation.

10. Create a relaxing pre-sleep routine.

11. If you do nap, have it earlier in the day.

12. Eat a lighter evening meal; don't eat within 2 hours of bedtime.

Recommended Books

Sleep Smarter: 21 Essential Strategies to Sleep Your Way to a Better Body, Better Health, and Bigger Success, by Shawn Stevenson

Sleep Soundly Every Night, Feel Fantastic Every Day, by Robert Rosenberg

STRESS MANAGEMENT

As you might imagine, chronic stress is connected with physical pain. Feeling stressed out on a regular basis compromises your immune system, wreaks havoc with your digestion, raises blood pressure, causes muscles to tighten and spasm, and disrupts sleep. It also causes or worsens mood disorders such as anxiety and depression. And of course there is that vicious cycle: Pain causes stress and stress negatively impacts pain. That is why it is imperative to develop strategies for stress reduction.

Recommended Books

The Relaxation and Stress Reduction Workbook, by Martha Davis, Elizabeth Robbins Eshelman and Matthew McKay

The Mayo Clinic Guide to Stress-Free Living, by Amit Sood

A Mindfulness-Based Stress Reduction Workbook, by Bob Stahl and Elisha Goldstein

Stress Management for Dummies, by Allen Elkin

Why Zebras Don't Get Ulcers: The Acclaimed Guide to Stress, Stress-Related Diseases, and Coping, by Robert Sapolsky

TAI CHI

An ancient form of Chinese exercise, tai chi consists of performing a series of slow, gentle movements accompanied by deep breathing. Tai chi is low impact and puts minimal stress on joints and muscles. Research is showing that there are many benefits to doing tai chi regularly, including:

1. Reduced stress

2. Improved mood

3. Increased energy and stamina

4. Improved balance and flexibility

5. Increased muscle strength

6. Enhanced sleep quality

7. Reduction of joint and muscle pain

8. Strengthend bones

So if you are suffering pain due to osteoarthritis, rheumatoid arthritis, fibromyalgia, headaches or back issues, tai chi is something to consider. And because many adult education centers offer classes, this option is easily accesible and affordable.

VITAMINS and MINERALS

Deficiencies in certain nutrients can lead to chronic pain. For example, low zinc is associated with joint and hip problems. A deficiency in magnesium can lead to a variety of physical and mental issues, including muscle soreness and cramping, joint pain, back aches, neck and head pain, and anxiety.

It's important to note that many dark colored sodas contain posphates, a type of chemical that binds with magnesium in the digestive tract, making it unavailable to the body (by inhibiting its absorption). So if you decide to add magnesium to your diet but drink soda, you will probably still remain deficient.

Vitamin D is a steroid hormone that humans produce naturally when we are in the sun. Unfortunately, most of us are still lack healthy levels of this substance. The consequences of a D deficiency include joint pain, general muscle pain and cramping, low energy and depression.

In order to find out if you have any vitamin or mineral deficiencies, ask your doctor to do a blood test.

Recommended Book

A-Z Guide to Drug-Herb-Vitamin Interactions, by Alan Gaby

YOGA

Originating in India, yoga is a physical and mental practice that uses body postures, breath work and meditation to create a state of health and relaxation. It is also a philosophical system with a spiritual component, although it is possible to practice yoga without incorporating that aspect.

Engaging in yoga, whether by oneself or in a class with a teacher, gets energy moving while strengthening and balancing out the body. Tighness means contracted muscles, which leads to compromised blood flow to those areas of the body. With gentle stretching those muscles begin to loosen and regain prior mobility and blood supply, leading to pain reduction. This also helps with reducing joint pain.

In addition, yoga's emphasis on relaxation and stress reduction is beneficial for reducing pain. Doing yoga regularly also improves sleep and mood, two important factors for a person living with chronic pain.

Recommended Books

Yoga for Pain Relief: Simple Practices to Calm Your Mind and Heal Your Chronic Pain, by Kelly McGonigal

Yoga for Depression: A Compassionate Guide to Relieve Suffering Through Yoga, by Amy Weintraub

Yoga for Emotional Balance: Simple Practices to Help Relieve Anxiety and Depression, by Bo Forbes

Yoga for Regular Guys: The Best Damn Workout on the Planet, by Diamond Dallas Page

Yoga for Beginners: 10 Super Easy Poses to Reduce Stress and Anxiety, by Peter Cook

Yoga Nidra for Complete Relaxation and Stress Relief, by Julie Lusk

OTHER RECOMMENDED BOOKS FOR PAIN MANAGEMENT

(that don't fall neatly into any of the above categories)

3 Minutes to a Pain-free Life: The Groundbreaking Program for Total Body Pain Prevention and Rapid Relief, by Joseph Weisberg

Full Catastrophe Living: Using the Wisdom of Your Mind and Body to Face Stress, Pain and Illness, by Jon Kabat-Zinn

Pain Free: A Revolucionary for Stopping Chronic Pain, by Pete Egoscue

Healing Back Pain: The Mind-Body Connection, by John Sarno

The Mindbody Prescription: Healing the Body, Healing the Pain, by John Sarno

Back in Control: A Surgeon's Roadmap Out of Chronic Pain, by David Hanscom

Stop Pain: Inflammation Relief for an Active Life, by Vijay Vad

Confronting Chronic Pain: A Pain Doctor's Guide to Relief, by Steven Richeimer

Be in Balance: A Simple Introduction to the Alexander Technique, by Angela Bradshaw

CHAPTER 14

Religion and Spirituality

Finding meaning in suffering. Feeling part of something bigger. Connecting to nature with awe.

Humility. Faith. Perspective.

Exploring your relationship with spirituality and religion is an important part of your recovery journey. This is because the belief in a higher power or force outside of oneself can give you the strenth to carry on during difficult times. It helps you make sense of what appears random and non-sensical. It allows you to recognize the sacred nature of life itself and your place in the universe.

I would argue that having transcendent experiences made possible through spiritual and religious practices are necessary for living a meaningful and satisfying life. Simply put, the deeper your connection to a power outside of yourself (however you might define that concept), the easier it will be for you to leave your addictions and compulsions behind.

The questions in this chapter are designed to make you think about what religion and spirituality mean to you, as well as their role in your daily life.

Please answer the following questions in your journal.

In your opinion, what is the difference between "religion" and "spirituality"? (if you're not sure, I've included definitions on page 183)

What does it mean "to have faith"?

What was your religious experience growing up?

What did your parents teach or show you about religion or spirituality?

Who else, if anyone, influenced you in terms of religion or spirituality?

How do your current religious or spiritual practices differ from those you had as a child?

Have you ever taken a break from or completely distanced yourself from your religious or spiritual practices? If so, why?

If you believe in God's existence, what is God like?

What do you think happens to us when we die?

What role, if any, does religion play in your life currently?

What role, if any, does spirituality play in your life currently?

Have you ever felt connected with something outside of yourself, like God, a Higher Power, another person, the Universe? When and where did/does that happen?

What has been your most profound spiritual experience? What made it so special?

Has there ever been a time in your life when you relied on religion, spirituality or faith for strength? What happened?

Who or what gives you strength and support during hard times?

Do you believe you have a soul or a deeper self? If so, how do you connect with it?

Do you ever feel that your soul or deeper self wants to communicate with you? If so, how does that typically happen?

How would you describe your relationship with your body? What could you do to deepen that relationship?

How would you describe your relationship with nature? What could you do to deepen that relationship?

Do you have a favorite hobby? What makes it special?

What music has touched your soul most deeply?

What book would you say has most deeply touched your soul?

To whom or what in your life do you feel a strong connection?

What group or community do you most feel a part of?

Are there any religious or spiritual practices that you do regularly?

What would you say is the most important ingredient for a spiritual or religious life?

If you had to pick the most sacred spot you've ever seen/been, what would that be?

Describe the time or activity that makes you feel the most connected to someone or something outside of yourself.

What do you do or where do you go to recharge your batteries?

What kinds of spiritual or religious activities would you like to do in the future, if any?

Is there any area of your religious or spiritual life you would like to explore or further develop?

Can you think of any religious or spiritual figures who you could use as a model for your future growth?

Do you have a daily spiritual or religious practice? If so, what is it and how does it make you feel? If not, is that something you would consider adding to your life? What would it be?

Do you have a weekly spiritual or religious practice? If so, what is it and how does it make you feel? If not, is that something you would consider adding to your life? What would it be?

What is the one thing you could add to your life that would deepen your spiritual connection?

Definitions

Religion: A specific and organized system of belief and worship, usually involving a moral code of ethics. The ceremonies, rules and rituals of a religion connect a person to a divinity or divinities.

Spirituality: The experience or expression of what is sacred. This also includes a person's experience of or belief in a power that exists outside of oneself. Spirituality can also be used to refer to a person's search for meaning, as well as a desire to be connected to forces outside of oneself.

Sacred: Something that is dedicated to a deity or to the worship of a deity. To be worthy of veneration, reverence, or religious respect. Holy.

Inventory #3

Let's take one more inventory of your life. How have things been going?

Sleep

1--10

Family Relationships

1--10

Intimate Relationship(s)

1--10

Relationship with Children

1--10

Physical Health

1--10

Mental Health

1--10

Relationship with God / Higher Power

1--10

Spirituality / Religion

1--10

Work/Career

1--10

Finances

1--10

Leisure Time / Relaxation

1--10

Hobbies / Things you do for fun

1--10

Food

1---10

Education / School

1---10

Relationships with Friends

1---10

Legal Issues

1---10

Energy Level

1---10

Optimism about the Future

1---10

For each area, in order to increase your score by just a single point, what can you:

Do more of?

Do less of?

Start?

Stop?

Check-in questions to answer in your journal:

How am I listening to my body?

How am I managing (and honoring) my daily rhythms?

How do I respond if I have made a poor choice?

How am I recovering if I have done something I regret?

How am I savoring my life?

How am I showing myself compassion?

How am I incorporating balance into my life?

How am I managing my emotions?

What have I given up in order to be healthy?

CONCLUSION

A jug fills drop by drop.

the Buddha

*Your difficulties are not obstacles on the path, they **are** the path.*

Ezra Bayda

Celebrate endings, for they precede new beginnings.

Jonathan Lockwood Huie

The ordinary arts we practice every day at home are of more importance to the soul than their simplicity might suggest.

Thomas Moore

There are only two ways to live your life. One is as though nothing is a miracle. The other is as though everything is a miracle.

Albert Einstein

There is no such thing as failure, only feedback.

NLP Supposition

YOU ARE THE AUTHOR OF YOUR OWN STORY

Thinking about the journey you have taken to get to this point in the book, how would you fill in the following?

This is a story of a --- who ---

Looking back on my life, I now understand ----

I will never understand ---

I have made peace with the fact that ---

In the future, I would like to be living a life in which I am ---

***

How have the roles you used to play in your life changed?

How has your relationship with fear changed?

How has your relationship with the expectations of others changed?

How has your past story influenced your new story?

What are you doing to empower yourself?

How has you relationship with spirituality changed? How have you been connecting with a Higher Power (however you might define that)?

What have you been doing to create happiness / peace / fulfillment in your life?

What is making your life meaningful?

What positive patterns are part of your life?

What five adjectives would you use to describe your current life?

What is working well for you in your new life? Why?

What obstacles have you overcome? How?

What have you released from your life that has freed up your energy?

What have you learned?

What skills have you developed?

What has gotten you through difficult times?

Whom have you forgiven? How did that make you feel?

What compromises have you made? Were they worth it?

What commitments have you made? With whom? How have those commitments served you?

***

What is your heart's desire? How are you honoring that every day?

***

And now I would like to leave you with a traditional Gaelic blessing. I wish you all the best on your journey to and through recovery. It's this long and winding road of self-discovery and healing that gives us everything we need to make the most of this precious life. Please remember to give yourself the credit you deserve for being courageous and doing the work.

Deep peace of the running wave to you

Deep peace of the flowing air to you

Deep peace of the quiet earth to you

Deep peace of the shining stars to you

Deep peace of the gentle night to you

Moon and stars pour their healing light on you

ABOUT THE AUTHOR

Andy Matzner is a licensed clinical social worker and psychotherapist in private practice. He also teaches psychology and mental health skills as a part-time professor at Virginia Western Community College. Andy is the author of *The Tarot Activity Book: A Collection of Creative and Therapeutic Ideas for the Cards* (2013) and *Everyone Has a Story: Using the Hero's Journey and Narrative Therapy to Reframe the Struggle of Mental Illness* (2015).

Made in the USA
Columbia, SC
19 August 2019